4D Strategies to

Living Unstuck

A guide to emotional intelligence
and managing expectations

by

John Polish

DEDICATIONS

This book is dedicated to three people who have had a profound impact on my life, and whose memory motivates me to drive-on at all costs.

To my mother, Ursula "Gail" Polish. I believe you would have been very proud of the work we have done at Unstuck. I can feel you looking down with a smile and a few smart remarks, which I miss very much.

To my daughter Abigail Anne Polish. You have made more of an impact in just 42 hours on Earth than I could hope to make in a lifetime. You are with me always and I am proud to be your dad.

To my friend and fellow Unstuck speaker, Dale Krause. I was blessed to have a friend that shared my vision for Unstuck. It is because of you that people across the country will be exposed to Unstuck. Hope you're finding Heaven as awesome as you found Earth.

CONTENTS

ACKNOWLEDGMENTS

I would like to thank all the speakers who have shared the stage at an Unstuck Happiness Conference. Your stories have inspired me as well as the audiences. I am grateful for your friendship. A special thank you to Sheryl Green for all your hard work and support with Unstuck.

Thanks to MVP Films. Dana and Monickie Scott, thanks for sharing the vision and turning Unstuck into a documentary film.

I want to show my appreciation to Michael Hauge for giving me the idea of relating the content in this book to Hollywood and for introducing me to Mark Travis. To Mark Travis and Elsha. You are truly a blessing. It was an honor to learn from you. Thank you for the drama chapter.

To my friends at the National Speakers Association. Great things happen when you surround yourself with great people.

Thank you to my family and friends who have supported and encouraged me.

And a special thanks to Toni Lynn for loving and believing in me.

John Polish

Introduction

What could you accomplish if there was nothing holding you back? I love to watch young children so filled with dreams and ambitions. One day they want to be an astronaut, the next day a firefighter. Children see possibilities where adults see limitations. It is up to the adults to teach them what they cannot do. But what if everything we were taught was a lie? What if we could be astronauts? Okay maybe not astronauts, but what if we didn't have to worry about our limitations? How much better would your life be if you had the power to overcome any obstacle, personally and professionally?

I may not have the power to make all your wishes come true, but I have found a way to systematize the process of getting unstuck from any, and all circumstances. I know that sounds like a serious claim, and it is. Skepticism would be an appropriate response right about now. But bear with me as I dig into the bold claim I just made. I am not a magician, or a genie in a bottle. I am just a regular guy who has had to face some very difficult circumstances. It is those struggles that have made me who I am today. I believe this is true for all of us.

I would be willing to bet that you are not the same person you were ten years ago. And you will not be the same ten years from now. As we go through life we are constantly learning new things and experiencing new things. We develop a greater understanding of who we are and what makes us happy.

I am certainly not the same person I was ten years ago. I used to believe that success was the key to happiness. I spent most of my life trying to figure out how to be successful so that I could be happy. Looking back, I can see how much I missed out on. I thought that I needed to stay on track and keep pushing towards my goals. If I stopped to have fun I might get derailed. It might prevent me from finding that success that awaits me. I even became judgmental of those who were not as driven as me. I thought they would end up living miserable lives because they are not working hard to succeed.

It took many years and some very painful experiences before I realized that I was the one who had been living a miserable life. I was doing everything I could to avoid my biggest fear, being stuck. I refused to settle for anything less than what I had convinced myself was the perfect life. I did not have a bad life. I just knew I was not living the life I wanted. Just like most people I work with today, I looked at happiness as something to achieve. What I discovered is that we all have exactly what we need to live a happy life. It may be buried beneath a pile of hurts, hang-ups, and heartaches, but it's in there. It took some horrible tragedies for me to finally realize that what I was searching for was a fantasy. I never would have believed that it would take three separate tragedies; a car accident and losing my mother and then my daughter seven months apart, for me to gain the perspective I needed to find happiness. My experience was painful. I was stuck for a long time. But I learned some invaluable lessons along the way that I am about to share with you. In the process of getting unstuck I let go of the illusion of a fantasy lifestyle, and what I found was even greater. The perfect life does not exist. The life I am living now is far from perfect, but it is wonderful.

My constant pursuit to find success led me to something greater. I found happiness and a peace that surpasses understanding. I may not walk around with a huge smile on my face all the time, but I am happy. I am happy because I know that my life has purpose. And I have learned how to conquer my greatest fear, being stuck.

I discovered that being stuck is a state of mind. It is real, but it is created by you. You get to set the expectations for your life. And you get to decide how long you will sit in your misery when you are not getting what you want. You have the power to get unstuck.

My life has purpose and that purpose is to help others learn how to live unstuck lives. I have taken the lessons I learned and created the 4 D strategies to living unstuck. Learn how to apply these 4D strategies and you can live like there is nothing holding you back;

1. Deal with your unmet expectations.
2. Define your ideals.
3. Develop your faith
4. Drive-on.

These strategies are designed to help you process your emotions. Keep in mind that we are all the sum of our 3 E's; education, experiences and emotional intelligence. We are defined not just by what has happened in our lives, but how we have responded. This book will help you understand the emotions that motivate you and the emotions that keep you stuck in your circumstances.

By applying the 4 D strategies you will be able to process your emotions quickly and get back to moving in the direction of your dreams. You will find confidence and the belief that everything will work out, regardless of your situation. Your circumstances do not have to dictate your happiness. I find myself fascinated with how people respond to similar circumstances, what inspires one person is devastating to another.

Can you imagine how drastically your life would change if you lost the use of a body part? My friend Eddie Garcia talks about going into hospital rooms to consult patients who have lost a body part. He told me the story of a guy who had his finger cut off in a construction accident. The man was devastated. He was visibly upset about losing his finger. Okay, to be honest I think I would be pretty upset too. Apparently, the man was very angry and was engulfed in self-pity, until Eddie came walking into the room.

It is hard to feel sorry for yourself after spending time around Eddie. In 2013 Eddie contracted a flesh-eating-bacteria. To save his life they had to amputate both hands and feet. When Eddie comes walking into the room with prosthetic feet and no hands suddenly the loss of a finger seems minor in comparison. But what is truly amazing about Eddie is his disposition. He is a very happy person who does not let his disability control his emotions. Eddie loves life and it shows. He still coach's youth basketball, softball and soccer. When he contracted the flesh-eating bacteria, he was not endowed with any super powers, at least not to my knowledge. What he did, without consciously knowing it, was apply the strategies we are discussing in this book.

Eddie is just one of many friends who have stories of tragedy and triumph. Since I entered the arena of public speaking I have been surrounded by amazing people with great stories to tell. Being around them has confirmed that what I say in this book is true. The processes discussed in here are what have set apart the stuck from the unstuck.

I knew that I had to find a way to showcase all these amazing stories to show people that they do not have to stay stuck in their circumstances. I began hosting the Unstuck Happiness Conferences in 2016. The conferences bring together people who have faced adversity and have emerged as leaders. Our speakers have faced all kinds of tragedies, but they refused to let their circumstances dictate their happiness.

The idea for the conference came to me after hearing many people that I care about say that they were stuck. They were stuck for a variety of different reasons but they all admitted that they were stuck. I have empathy for people who are stuck, having spent most of my adult life feeling stuck myself. I also know what it is like to live unstuck. I love knowing that I have the power to determine the direction of my life. We have heard it said that happiness is in the journey and not the destination. When you are stuck you are unable to move, there is no journey! That is why it is impossible to feel stuck and happy at the same time. When you are living an unstuck life, you are free to move in the direction of your dreams and there is nothing restricting your movement. Just knowing that you are free to pursue your dreams makes it possible to feel happy again.

Once I figured out how to get myself moving again, a whole new world has presented itself to me. My passion has led me to help others who are stuck. What started as a passion has become a mission. I have dedicated my life to helping people learn to live unstuck.

What my work has revealed to me is that we all get stuck. We get stuck for a million different reasons, but the strategies for getting unstuck are very similar. The steps we take to process our emotions are the same regardless of how we got stuck. Sometimes the process is instinctive and requires very little thought. Other times the process must be very intentional and can take a long time, but it is still very much the same process. By learning this process, you will be better equipped to recognize when you are at risk of being stuck, and how to move beyond your circumstances. My strategies are very simple, but they are not easy.

Chapter 1

What does it mean to be stuck?

Before we can even begin to think about the process of getting unstuck, we must first learn to identify what it means to be stuck. You may have gotten your car stuck in the mud or snow. You may have had your hand stuck in a door jam, or seen a dog get his head stuck in a fence. Have you had your tongue stuck on a frozen pole? Or your head stuck in a honey tree? Those are literal examples of being physically stuck. They demonstrate an inability to move.

According to the Cambridge Dictionary being stuck means that you are unable to move from a particular position or place; or unable to change a situation. When we say that we are stuck we are admitting that we are unable to advance towards our goals or desired destination. We all get stuck. How long you stay stuck and how much work will be necessary to get you moving again are determined by the value you place on the outcome and the severity of the circumstances.

Have you ever been stuck in traffic? Of course, we all have. Being stuck in traffic means that I am not able to move towards my destination at my desired rate of speed. There have been times when I was stuck in traffic and it was no big deal. There have also been times when I was stuck in traffic and became extremely frustrated or angry. The difference was the importance I placed on the result. In other words, what was going to be the consequence of not arriving at my destination on time? If I knew that I was not going to miss anything important by arriving a few minutes late then it was much easier to deal with slow traffic. Conversely, if I knew that the consequence would be painful I was much more emotional about the delay. Being late for work could result in a write up or docked pay, that makes the traffic jam more emotional to deal with. The traffic delay created an unmet expectation. I expected to be on time, now that is not going to happen. My level of discontent is in direct proportion to the value I placed on the expectation.

While we may place a high value on the outcome associated with the traffic jam example we would have to agree that the severity of a traffic jam is minimal in comparison to many other circumstances we face. Meaning, the likelihood of it happening is greater and has less shock value associated with it. A terminal medical diagnosis, loss of a loved one, a divorce, an addiction and losing your job are all examples of a more severe circumstance.

You may have severe circumstances with differing levels of value. Divorce is considered a severe circumstance, but I was much more impacted by my parents' divorce than I was by the divorce of Brad and Angelina. When you have a severe circumstance and a high value, those situations usually require a concentrated effort to get unstuck and moving again.

This is a slight adaptation of the impact/probability chart that is widely used in risk management. The premise is that if something has a low impact and low probability of happening you are only monitoring the situation to see if it becomes more likely to happen. The greater the impact and probability, the more a strategic focus is necessary.

In our assessment, when faced with a situation that has a low severity and a low value the process is almost instinctive. It requires little to no effort to get moving again. The higher the value and the higher the severity, the more of a strategic focus will be needed to overcome. This means that you will need to be intentional about moving through the process. It will take effort and time. This book provides you the strategies, you supply the focus.

In my first book, "Finding Your Happiness", I explained the Personal Happiness Graph and how it works. It is a tool I created to allow you to see how happy you are in the five essential categories which encompass all your expectations. It allows you to see the difference between your ideal self and your actual self. Your level of discontent is determined by the difference between the two. In other words, you are unhappy when you do not have what you want in those five areas. As long as you can see that you are making progress and narrowing that gap then it is easy to stay motivated and moving. You begin to feel stuck when you realize that you are not getting any closer to what you want, or when something you value has been taken from you. You are stuck because you have an expectation that is unmet, and you do not feel like you are going to be able to meet that expectation.

You say you are stuck in a rut it means that your routine is boring and feels like the same old thing. You use the word stuck because the expectation might be that you will live an exciting life filled with purpose and adventure. If you are stuck in a job you do not like, or an unfulfilled marriage, or a financial situation, you are saying that you expected things to be different, and you do not feel like you are making enough progress towards realizing your expectation.

Often, you find yourself stuck because of a series of choices you have made, but there are times when events happen which will instantly change your situation. When tragedy strikes it often picks you up and moves you far from the life you desired. It rarely happens that your car slides off the road into a pile of money, or you fall down and get up better looking than before you fell. The things that happen in an instant and change your life forever are usually not the things you want to happen. But as you get better at applying the 4 D strategies you will learn to be thankful for the events that have changed the course of your life.

I have spent much of my life as an athlete and a coach. In 2002 I was coaching high school football. I enjoyed running around with the kids. I would run sprints with the team and race against them. Even at 31 years old I could still hold my own. That came to an end on October 27th of 2002. I was driving home when a car pulled out in front of me. A car was turning into my lane on the wrong side of a meridian strip. I swerved to avoid the car and hit a light pole head on. My leg shot through my pelvis. I shattered my pelvis and crushed my nerve. I have not run a sprint since. My life was changed forever in an instant. To this day I cannot control my toes on my right foot. I cannot feel the difference between hot and cold, or sharp and dull on that foot. I live with pain every day. It wasn't like I had written out goals to run sprints, or to be able to tell when I am standing on a 100-degree surface, I just expected that I would be able to.

After the accident I was told that I would never walk again. How could this be? I was an athlete I needed my legs. When I was told that I would not walk again I was stuck, (no pun intended). I was emotionally stuck. I felt sorry for myself. I really had no idea how I would be able to adapt to life if I could not walk. I did okay in the hospital for about a month. When I got home the frustration kicked in instantly. I began to feel depressed. I didn't want to get out of bed. I stayed in bed for days. Then one day, I decided to change my emotional state. I crutched my way to the kitchen and made myself breakfast. It may not sound like a big deal, but to me that was like running a marathon. I realized at that moment that life would go on whether I was walking or not. No amount of feeling sorry for myself would heal me. It wasn't easy, but I kept moving. I had lost motivation because I was focused on what I could not do. Unfortunately, I know people who are still stuck because of an unmet expectation from years ago.

I believe that making the decision to not allow myself to be stuck, contributed to the success of my rehabilitation. By having the proper mindset, I was able to maximize my efforts during physical therapy. I never missed a session, though some days were harder than others. I believe that there were some emotional and physical benefits to choosing a positive mindset as well. Had I accepted what the doctor told me, I may not be walking today.

I understand that there are some horrible things that happen. I know that we have all been wounded and we have the scars to show for it. Those scars serve as reminders. I am not suggesting that you forget what has happened and move on. Quite the contrary. What I am saying is that the emotional attachment we have to our circumstances is what keeps us stuck. I am suggesting that we learn strategies to effectively process our emotions. I endorse that we stay attached to those emotions that have made us who we are, but that we do not need to stay stuck in them either. Throughout this book you will learn strategies that will help you be able to process your emotions in a healthy manner.

You may be reading this thinking that we are talking a lot about processing feelings and emotional touchy-feely things and this is not for you. Good it's not for me either. In fact, it is very common for people to not want to talk about their feelings, especially men. There is actually a condition known in psychiatry as normative male alexithymia. According to Psychology Today, Gregg Henriques Ph.D. (November 14, 2014) wrote that this is a personality construct characterized by the subclinical inability to identify and describe emotions in the self. It is found in 10% of males.

We are all impacted by our circumstances. Failure to deal with your emotions properly will certainly cause problems in your life. It may not happen immediately, but it will eventually surface. It will begin to affect your work and your relationships. You may also notice physiological changes to your body as a result. Holding on to your emotions, knowingly or not, sends a signal to your body that it is in distress. This could result in several health-related issues. By learning the strategies to deal with your emotions you will be able to get back on track quicker and avoid adding health problems to your list of concerns.

Some people get stuck because they fail to acknowledge that there is an issue that needs to be dealt with. Others get stuck because they are too focused on the issue. The key is to recognize when you are at risk of being stuck, so you can turn and move in a new direction.

The most successful people in the world have one thing in common. It is not that they don't face difficulties. It is that they have learned to pivot. They recognize when a change needs to be made. Sometimes they need to change what they are doing, to get what they want. And other times they need to change what they want, because they realize it is unobtainable. Successful people pivot quickly. They turn and move in a new direction. Others stare at the problem wondering where it all went wrong.

I have found that very few people have the skills necessary to be able to navigate through trials and tragedies and come out unscathed. I was never one of those people that liked to talk about touchy-feely things. I was good at stuffing my feelings and moving on. And for a long time that worked for me. I was an athlete. I learned how to shake it off and get back in the game. As a football player there were times (rare as they were) that I would get beat on a play. The guy across from me would get the better of me. Of course, I was frustrated and mad. I thought about what went wrong and how I would have to do better the next time. I found that I did a lot of that internal processing with my head down feeling bad. However, I knew that if I didn't pick my head up, he would beat me on the next play too, and like it or not the next play was coming.

This mental processing worked well for me for a long time. I never stayed down for long and I did not allow little things to get to me. In fact, I would say that this is an effective strategy much of the time. I learned to temper my emotions. I would not get too excited about anything, but I would not get too upset either. I just buried my feelings and moved on. However, when it comes to those severe circumstances, moving on without effectively processing can be detrimental. There came a time when I could not stuff anymore down.

I thought that car accident would be my defining moment. I was told I would not walk again and I proved them wrong. Hard work and dedication paid off. Of course, I had permanent damage and pain to live with, but I didn't get stuck. It would take a lot more than a car accident to keep me down. Indeed, it did!

I got married in 2008. Three months to the day, my wife informed me that she was expecting. My first baby was on the way. I was going to be a dad. I was so happy! I lived across country from my family and I could not wait to call them. It was the happiest I had heard my mom in years. She even called me back that night to tell me that she just knew I was going to have a girl and she could not wait to watch me have to deal with that for the next 18 years.

Little did I know, that would be the last conversation I would ever have with my mother. Less than 36 hours later she would die of a sudden heart attack at the age of 54. That was not supposed to happen. My expectation was that my mom would be there when my baby was born. This was not part of the plan. I was upset over the loss of my mom. I experienced the emotions we will discuss in another chapter; fear, frustration, anger and depression. But who has time for that. I quickly shifted my focus from the loss of my mom, to the arrival of my daughter. I was way too happy about becoming a dad to live in mourning for my mom. The Bible tells us that there is a time to rejoice and a time to cry. I had both happening simultaneously, so I chose to rejoice.

I felt pretty good about how I handled the situation. I was able to stay focused on what needed to be done. I stayed level headed and got back to normal quickly. But this was not like getting beat on a football play, this was the loss of my mother. However, I treated it the same. Shake it off and get back in the game!

Truth be told, there were many emotions that I had not dealt with pertaining to the loss of my mother. The fear, frustration, anger and depression began to surface in the coming months. I was also living with a great deal of guilt. For more than eleven years I had been living across country. When she passed I felt like a horrible son. I didn't get back home to see her nearly enough. I was still in that mode of trying to be successful and I know she sensed that I was not happy. Our final conversation was the first time she felt my happiness. I never took the time to process the emotions attached to my mom's passing, and

I certainly was not prepared to deal with what was about to happen.

On April 20th, 2009, Abigail Anne Polish was born. I was a dad! The moment I had been waiting a lifetime for was here. Unfortunately, I did not get to fully enjoy the arrival of my daughter. We found out the day before we delivered that she tested positive for a genetic disorder Trisomy 18. It was terminal. We delivered Abby and held her for 42 hours before she passed.

During that time, I experienced every emotion known to man, the good the bad and the ugly. It would take another book to explain to you all the emotions I felt during that time. What I can tell you is that my ex-wife and I handled our emotions the best we could. We took the time to enjoy Abby. We went into it knowing that our time with her would be limited and that we wanted to make the most of every moment. I was a proud father. I was also very proud of how we handled all the emotions that surrounded us during the time she was with us, and even shortly after her passing.

My life would never be the same. Unfortunately, I handled life the only way I knew how at the time. Shake it off and get back in the game! I went right back to work and attempted to get life back to "normal" as quickly as possible. This time it was much different. I was now responsible for my family and not just for myself. I had a wife, a step-daughter, in-laws and my own family. Everyone was handling the loss in their own way, the best they could, but each differently. I wanted to get back to normal, but there was no normal. Life was forever changed.

Without giving too much away I can tell you that not learning to process emotions would cost me everything. I would soon hit rock bottom before seeking the answers to living an unstuck life. My journey was hard and painful. My experience was invaluable. Short of having my daughter here today I would not trade my experience for anything in the world.

It took sitting alone in my misery and grieving my daughter, my mother, and my marriage, to be the catalyst for change. Change that was long overdue. I later came to the realization that I had spent my entire life being afraid of living stuck. For two decades I told myself that I was going to pursue my dreams and would live the life that I wanted. What my research has taught me was that I was not running towards my dreams, instead I was running from my fears. I was afraid of being stuck.

Being stuck means that you are not free to pursue your dreams. You are being held back by the emotions that result from an unmet expectation. Your definition of being stuck will be different than mine, or anyone else's for that matter, because you have different dreams than I do. What I consider stuck may be your ideal. What makes the strategies universal is the fact that the emotions are the result of an inability to move towards your ideal, at your desired rate of speed, regardless of what that ideal may be.

Today, I have applied what I have learned, and I have packaged my experiences into this message. I am now living a life I never dreamt possible. I have some amazing people in my life. My work has purpose and meaning. I get to do things I never imagined before. I have a relationship with my daughter. She may not be here physically, but she is the reason for everything that I do. I say that every day is take your daughter to work day. I have a whole new life and an amazing new wife to share it with. This life would have never been possible had I not learned and applied the concepts I am sharing in this book.

The 4 D strategies to living unstuck have given me a new perspective and have opened doors to an amazing lifestyle. My prayer for you is that these strategies will have the same impact on your life.

Chapter 2

Expectations

Expectations are the root of all of our hurts, hang-ups and heartaches.

Expectations are defined as a strong belief that something will happen or should happen. There is a difference between wanting and expecting. Expectations are based on historical evidence. Your education and experiences have led you to a conclusion regarding your desired outcome. The greater the probability of the outcome, the more likely you are to expect that outcome.

For example, it is common for new couples to "want" a baby. Once a woman becomes pregnant we say that she is "expecting". This is because our education and experience have taught us that a pregnancy will last around 40 weeks, and at the end of said pregnancy there will be a baby. Once she learns she is pregnant she shifts from wanting a baby to expecting one.

There is nothing wrong with wanting something. You can want something without expecting. I have lived in Las Vegas for twenty years now. Millions of people travel here every year and most of them want to win millions of dollars while they are visiting. Many want to win so badly that they will sit at a slot machine for hours hoping to hit the jackpot. There have certainly been many people who have hit the jackpot in Las Vegas. Hearing the stories of people who have won millions has helped create that want which so many tourists experience. If you were to come to Las Vegas expecting to hit the jackpot we would think you were crazy. According to Slot Machine resource in Las Vegas, (http://www.slot-machine-resource.com/ megabucks) the odds of hitting Megabucks are greater than 1 in 17 million. It would be delusional to expect to beat those odds.

Not all expectations begin with a deep desire. Expectations are developed as a result of your education and experiences. Each of us have expectations that we have never given any thought to, we just expect because that is the way it has always been, it is the natural order of things. I didn't say that I wanted to run sprints, I just expected I would be able to. I did not expect that a car accident would cause permanent damage leaving me unable to run. Nobody expects to get cancer, we just assume we will be healthy.

Tragedies often result in unmet expectations because they disrupt what we have taken for granted. Something we did not expect to happen has happened, leaving us with a feeling of loss. There is now a gap between what we want and what we have. We may never have taken the time to express what we wanted, it may have been implied.

There is power in an expectation that does not exist when we want or hope. I hope to finish this book by the end of the month, or I expect to be done by the end of the month? There is much more power in the expectation. It implies a certain level of dedication necessary to complete the book. Would you rather hear your surgeon tell you that he expects the surgery to go just fine and he expects a full recovery, or that he wants the surgery to go fine and he hopes you have a full recovery? There is power in the expectation, due mostly to the fact that the expectation is based on our education and previous experiences. We expect because history predicts for us what the most likely outcome will be.

There is great value in having clearly defined expectations. Your expectations can serve as your main source of motivation. By clearly stating what you expect you begin to see the path to get to your desired outcome. The most successful people do not just want to succeed they expect to succeed. This expectation motivates them to do whatever is necessary to reach their goal. Everyone wants to succeed but few have taken the time to develop a crystal-clear picture of what that success looks like. It is much easier to walk in confidence when you expect rather than hope. When you hope, or want, to succeed it appears you have left room for doubt. If you are going to play, go all in. We will talk more about how to do this in the chapter, Defining Your Ideals.

In 1964 Victor H. Vroom of the Yale School of Management created the Expectancy Theory of Motivation. (www.valuebasedmanagement.net/methods_vroom_expect ancy_theory.html). The idea is that people will make choices to gain pleasure or avoid pain. The choices we make are in direct correlation to the results we expect to get. He discovered that all employees had different expectations and different beliefs about their own abilities. He determined that people would be motivated to perform as long as they believed that their effort would produce the desired result and that the result would satisfy a need that was strong enough to warrant the level of performance. If they did not believe in the purpose of their work, or in their ability to successfully complete the task, they would not remain motivated for long. In other words, if you want something bad enough, and you believe that your effort will be enough to accomplish what you want, then you will find the motivation you need.

We have talked about what it means to expect to succeed. The harsh reality of life is that many of us expect to fail. Experience has taught us that success is hard. We have learned to tell ourselves that we are not good enough, we do not have what it takes, we lack the resources. There are plenty of lies that we tell ourselves on a regular basis which limit our belief in self.

Henry Ford was credited with saying; "whether you think you can or whether you think you can't you're right." While I could argue that there are people who think they can do things that they either cannot or should not do, there is a lot of truth to the fact that if you think you can't you are right. Negative self-talk will destroy any hopes and dreams you have. In the chapter on developing your faith we will teach you how you can safeguard against negative self-talk.

Take the time to evaluate your expectations. Where do they come from? Are they realistic? Is there evidence that what you expect can actually happen? Throughout this book I will share strategies to help you live an unstuck life. In order to live an unstuck life, you must believe that what you want is obtainable.

While there is great power in having an expectation, there is also a great sense of disappointment you feel when that expectation goes unmet. It is one thing to not get what you want. Not getting what you expect will result in an even greater sense of pain. Think about the times when you expected things to turn out one way and they did not. Maybe you expected to get a promotion and were passed up. Maybe you expected a business deal to go through and it fell apart in the final moments. Did you expect to have a great marriage, only to have your partner leave you? I expected to bring my daughter home from the hospital after she was born. The greater the expectation, the greater the disappointment when it goes unmet.

I spent most of my adult life searching for happiness. I also said that all of our hurts, hang-ups and heartaches are caused by our expectations. One of the reasons I was unhappy for so long was because I had such high expectations. I had high expectations in all areas of my life. I suffered from the same problem that many young people have today. I could see myself as a success. I could visualize having all the things that I wanted. The problem was that I had no idea what it would take to achieve my goals. I had expectations that were not based on education or experience. Now I use the Personal Happiness Graph to help me assess my expectations. If there is a large gap between what I want and what I have, I take the time to try and figure out why. Rather than beat myself up over what I don't have, I start by looking at what I want. I might find a milestone that will get me closer to what I want and set that as the expectation, making it more reasonable to obtain. This reduces the stress I put on myself.

One of the dangers of having such high expectations for yourself is that you run the risk of becoming very judgmental. It is important to remember that we all want different things. That is what makes life so interesting. Holding others to my own standards also contributed to much of my discontent. I was so judgmental of everyone around me that it held me back from having meaningful relationships. I just assumed that there was a right and a wrong way to live and when people were not doing what I thought was right I would distance myself from them. As you could imagine it was pretty lonely at the top.

I have spent time in some very rich exclusive neighborhoods, and in some extremely poor villages. Some of the poorest places I have been to have had some of the happiest people. This is because their expectations were more relational and less materialistic. They didn't need as much in order to be happy. As a result, there was less of a gap between their ideal and their actual.

Have you ever heard the phrase, "peace that surpasses understanding'? I used to think that was religious speak. I have read it in the Bible and heard it in many sermons. The basic premise is that in difficult times God will grant you peace, even in the midst of the storm. I have experienced this peace twice in my life. The first time was after my car accident. I was in excruciating pain, but I had peace. The other time was in the hospital delivering Abby. During the two worst times in my life I experienced the most peace. Yes, I do believe that there was divine intervention. But all divine intervention is, is us getting out of our own way and letting God do His work. What did it mean for me to get out of my own way? I can tell you this much, during those times I was not thinking about paying bills. I did not wish I had a bigger house or a nicer car. The only expectations I had were to heal, and to have the people I cared most about with me. To me that divine intervention was God telling me not to want for anything. He was telling me that I had everything I needed, and He would help me get through this.

I think it is often easier to get through tragedies because we are more focused on what is important. It was after those tragedies, when life got back to "normal", that things began falling apart. Looking back, it was almost as if I could see myself turning to God and saying, "thanks but I got it from here." In an instant we go right back to what we want and expect from ourselves and others.

Most if not all disagreements between people are a direct result of an unmet expectation. It is one thing to have high expectations for yourself. When you project expectations on others you leave yourself open for disappointment and even heartache. We are constantly putting expectations on others. Children expect their parents to provide for them. Spouses expect their significant other to love them and to stay faithful. We expect teachers to teach and police to protect. Children expect Santa to bring them toys. We expect good service in restaurants. She expects help with the dishes. He expects to be able to unwind and watch television. I could go on for days about expectations that we all have. The next time you find yourself in a disagreement with someone you care about, stop and think about what expectations you both had that went unmet. By understanding one another's expectations, you will gain a new perspective. This could stop a lot of fights from happening.

Understanding expectations is the first step to developing emotional intelligence. It is not bad to have expectations. The key to finding happiness is learning to manage your expectations. It begins with acknowledging that negative emotions are the result of an unmet expectation.

Chapter 3

Emotions

Emotions are what keeps life interesting. We would not know what we like or dislike, if not for our emotions. When we experience something that we like we feel an emotional high. When we experience something we don't like we feel an emotional low. We are constantly experiencing highs and lows and to varying degrees. It is the highs and lows that make us feel alive. It is natural to want to enjoy the highs and avoid the lows. In reality they are interdependent. Without the lows we would not be able to appreciate the highs. And the highs are necessary for us to be able to process the lows.

Your emotional well-being is not determined by a snapshot in time. It is the result of your ability to manage your emotions over long periods of time. Think of your feelings like a picture. And think of your emotional well-being like it is a video of your life. It is ok to have a negative emotion. What is not ok is to sit in that emotion for so long that it begins to make up your emotional well-being. You can have negative feelings without becoming a negative person. The same is true for positive emotions. You can do things that make you feel good, but that does not necessarily mean you will have a positive emotional well-being. In the chapter Deal with Your Unmet Expectations, we will discuss positive psychology and how you can take action towards developing a positive well-being that will sustain.

Understanding your emotions will help you to make better decisions. Your emotions serve as your experience filters. Emotions are feelings that you get to let you know how to process an experience. You determine if an experience is good or bad, based on the emotions you feel in those circumstances. For example, I do not like coconut. I don't like the smell, the texture or the taste. Coconut is an ingredient that is used in many different recipes. It is not necessary for me to try every recipe to determine if I will like it or not, if it contains coconut I can declare that I do not like it before even tasting it.

I like when my wife kisses me. My wife likes her coconut lip gloss. Even though I know I like her kisses, I also know that I do not like the smell of coconut. This is an example of good verse evil. Sometimes I want the kiss enough to endure the coconut and other times, I have to ask her to wash it off first. Right or wrong, we make decisions based on the experiences we expect to feel.

We tend to file our experiences away in our memory banks. When faced with a similar circumstance we're able to recall the emotion we felt in the previous experience. If you experience pain when you hit your thumb with a hammer, chances are you will be more careful the next time you swing a hammer, in order to avoid the pain you previously experienced. The same is true for positive feelings. If you laugh the first time you watch a television sitcom there is a high probability you will watch another episode.

Because of our experiences we are able to feel something without going through the actual circumstances. My wife can see the name of a restaurant and determine that it is her new favorite restaurant before she ever steps foot in the place. This is because she makes associations. She draws on similar experiences to determine if she will like something. In her case, she has a dairy allergy, so when she sees a new vegan restaurant she has already decided she is a fan. Even though she is not a vegan herself, she knows there will be plenty of non-dairy options for her. She is having an experience in her mind before she visits the restaurant. I am much more of a skeptic, but thus far her intuition has served her well.

The Franklin Institute in Philadelphia offers an experience with virtual reality technology. They have concluded that "your brain builds on your past experiences to develop "rules" by which to interpret the world." (https://www.fi.edu/virtual-reality?) We now have devices that will simulate an experience for you. By wearing the virtual reality goggles, you can have an experience almost as if it were happening in real life. If you go on Youtube you can search hundreds of videos of people who end up breaking something because of an emotional reaction they have while wearing virtual reality goggles. This happens because of their experience filters.

Your emotions also serve as a moral compass. You're able to determine right from wrong based on the emotions that surround the circumstance. If you watch the news you will see many stories of injustice. You will see people who have been abused, robbed, assaulted, even murdered. We have all been hard wired to have a negative emotion when we see stories like those.

I live in Las Vegas. As I write this we are just a few months removed from the October 1, 2017 massacre on the Las Vegas strip. The Route 91 Harvest Festival is a three-day country concert. I have been to this concert in the past, it was a great experience. It is an outdoor concert enjoyed by thousands. That is until some deranged man on the 32nd floor of a nearby hotel, decided to fire machine guns into the crowd. Fifty-eight people lost their lives that day.

Las Vegas is known as sin city. It has even been referred to as the devil's playground. It is a city that prides itself on blurring the line between right and wrong. On October 1st I sat and watched the news, outraged and devastated. (Just for the record, my experience is that Las Vegas is also grace city. There are some wonderful people here and it is in Las Vegas that I found a relationship with God.) However, I acknowledge the reputation the city has. The popular belief was that this city was morally corrupt.

On October 2nd I woke up in awe. I did not know what to do but I knew I had to do something. The news said there was a need for people to donate blood so that is what I was going to do. I waited in line for twelve hours over two days just to donate blood. Tens of thousands of people had the same response I had. They had to turn away donations of food and water because they had too much. In a city known for being morally corrupt I have not met a single person who was not outraged by the senseless act of violence that day.

I strongly believe that God has weaved into our DNA a moral code. That is why we all have negative emotions when we see injustice in this world. When we see events like the Route 91 harvest festival, or children being hurt, we have a strong emotional response because we have been hard wired to know right from wrong. We experience emotions appropriate to the situation. We hate injustice and we love the heroes journey. It is your emotions that remind you of what is morally right or wrong.

There are also health and safety benefits to understanding your emotions. Fear is an emotion that often steers us away from danger. Because you were afraid of getting hurt you took safety precautions. Fear of suffering causes us to seek medical checkups. Pain is an emotion that causes us to seek medical treatment. Often your negative emotions will work to keep you safe and healthy.

While negative emotions may cause us to seek treatment, they can also cause harm to our bodies if we allow ourselves to sit in those emotions for too long. Those negative emotions tell your body that it is in distress. Our bodies are designed to protect us from harm. When you feel stress, your body responds accordingly. Failure to deal with your negative emotions can lead to disease and other health related issues.

If you maintain a positive emotional well-being it can relieve your body of stress. It also motivates you to make healthier choices regarding food and exercise. There are many proven health benefits to maintaining a positive attitude.

It is more important now than ever in history to develop an emotional intellect. It is a bit ironic that emojis have become so popular. An emoji is a character, an image, that we use in electronic communication such as text messaging, to show the emotions we feel. There are literally hundreds of emojis we could use to show people how we are feeling. The ironic part is that I have watched as people text things like lol, (laugh out loud), and there is no actual laughter coming from them. They send a crying emoji and a virtual hug, with a straight face and no human contact. We are learning to fake emotions. Real emotional intelligence starts with the ability to recognize the onset of a real emotion and identify its cause.

The 4 D strategies we will discuss are all designed to help you process your emotions. By paying attention to how you feel and what causes you to feel a certain way you are developing the emotional awareness needed to process effectively.

Chapter 4

Distractions

In the beginning of the book we talked about what it means to be stuck. You have an expectation. The expectation is not met. This produces a negative emotion. The beginning of emotional intelligence is to recognize the onset of your emotions, then make wise decisions about what to do with your feelings. When your negative emotions kick in there are three things you could do;

1. Do nothing. Just ignore it, or shake it off and get back in the game.

2. Apply the 4 D strategies to process your emotions in a healthy way.

3. Look for distractions.

A distraction is anything that will take your mind off the unmet expectation so that you do not have to feel the negative emotions. It is a coping mechanism. A distraction gives you something else to focus on for a while. It helps you take your mind off things. It can also be a great tool for tempering emotions before they get out of control. Your hope is that as time passes the expectation becomes less important, rendering the emotion powerless over you. In other words, it works itself out.

There are times when a distraction is just what you need, and other times when it could be detrimental. A better understanding of your emotions will help you make wise decisions.

The way a distraction works is it shifts your focus to something else and before you know it, you forgot that you even had that negative feeling, or the feeling becomes less intense. Remember, when you are in the middle of the wreckage, all you can see is the smoke. That means that the feeling you have right now is always your most important feeling. As time passes that feeling fades. When you hit your thumb with a hammer all you can think about is the pain. An hour later it is as if it never happened.

The alternative to seeking distractions is to deal with the

issue right away. While this sounds like the healthier approach, it often is not. This is why counselors will tell you to take some time and calm down before discussing important issues with your spouse. It is why we are told to never spank your children while you are angry. Sometimes it is a good thing to take a timeout, seek a distraction to calm down from the emotion.

Taking a time out means that you are removing yourself from the situation for a set period of time. Hopefully, during that time you may realize that what seemed so important in the moment may not be as big of a deal as you thought. Timeouts must include a distraction, or a positive reinforcement. If you have a fight with your spouse and you take a time out and go into separate rooms just to think about how upset you are, it is no different than two boxers going to neutral corners between rounds. When the timeout is over you just come back swinging again.

Using positive reinforcements helps during the timeout period. Take the time to think about what is important to you, and how your current emotional state may prevent you from having what you want. I have never heard a single successful person give credit to their negative feelings or their bad attitude as being the reason for their success. I have heard them say that it was their inspiration, or their catalyst for change. It was the negative emotion that inspired them to get moving again.

I am sure most people are familiar with the concept of timeout, as it has become the number one strategy in disciplining children. In a recent article in Live Science, (https://www.livescience.com/55932-how-to-make-timeouts-work-for-your-kids.html) The Science of Timeouts: How to Make Them Work for Your Kids, the author discusses some of the mistakes parents make when issuing a timeout to children. I could not help but see the comparison to mistakes we make in seeking distractions.

The biggest mistake made in timeouts was not specifying the behavior. In much the same way, we often seek a distraction at the onset of the emotion without identifying why that emotion triggered us. In this case the distraction may work for a while only because you have forgotten what you were feeling. Since you were not aware of why you felt the way that you did, the negative emotion is certain to come back to you the moment something triggers your memory. In most relationships couples have something that they have recurring fights about. You have a disagreement, it may turn into a fight, then you find a distraction. You may take a timeout, or you may just agree to end the fight. Without addressing why, you had such an emotional response to stimuli it is certain to happen again. I know that I have had many disagreements that ended because both parties agreed that it was not worth ruining a relationship over. Because the expectation was never dealt with the fight did not end, it just went into remission. You can be certain rounds 2,3 and 4 are coming.

Another reason the timeout does not work is because the parent and child continue the dialog rather than ignoring the issue for the time period. The child whines and the parent responds. There is no appropriate time away from the circumstances. As adults we do this in the form of passive aggressive behavior. We say that we are okay and can move past a situation, but our action show that we have not let go of the expectation.

Other than just taking a timeout, it is important to look at how you are distracting yourself. When my mom died I had a pregnancy to distract me. Much like positive psychology, I focused on something good in hopes that the bad would go away. It did not go away, it resurfaced in other ways. The distraction did not work.

When I lost my daughter, I started running every day. I continued to go to church. I did a lot of positive things to try to forget about the negative feelings I was having. I thought that if I could stay positive then it would not hurt as bad. It still hurt.

I began to start focusing on what I did not have. I'm not just talking about my loss. There were other unmet expectations in my life. I shifted my focus, but all I did was shift from one unmet expectation to another. I was unhappy with my work. I was also unsatisfied with relationships in my life and my finances. I found a lot to be unhappy about. Because I did not want to focus on losing Abby, I focused on the other unmet expectations. Remember the longer you focus on something the bigger it seems.

Looking back, my biggest issue was that I felt alone and ill-equipped to handle the responsibilities I had. I was hurting but so was everyone around me. I could not seem to help myself, how was I supposed to help anyone else. I took on the victim mentality. I was hoping that someone would come along and fix everything. Part of the victim mentality is that you must have someone else to blame for your feelings. I projected my negativity onto my loved ones. Of course, they were all suffering too and were unable to help me. The healthy distractions were not working. I began to look for a way to vent my frustrations. I found my distraction online. I could complain about what I did not have and there were people that would give me the attention I was seeking. I did not know these people, never met any of them. But for a while I started to feel relevant again. I found people that would support my feelings, which naturally just created more resentment for my real-life situation.

Grief is real, and it is severe. There was no distraction in this world that was big enough to make me forget about Abby. Knowing what I know now about emotional intelligence, I am embarrassed to admit that I did the things I did to try to avoid dealing with the pain.

Distractions often start out harmless. It is when the negative emotions persist that the distractions become larger and more dangerous. What starts as a distraction often turns into another problem itself, such as addiction or other self-destructive acts.

I knew a young man who was a great athlete. He was a popular, good-looking kid with everything going for him. A tragedy nearly cost him his life. Overjoyed with the fact that he survived, he attempted to get back to life as normal as quickly as possible. Although he survived the tragedy and regained most of his normal function, he still had some fine motor skill problems. His gate was affected, and he was no longer able to run the way he had before. He had some balance issues that prevented him from competing in sports at the same level he had before his tragedy.

Rather than being grateful to be alive and adjusting to his life with new expectations, he continued to focus on the fact that he was not the same as he was before the tragedy. He wanted the same things he wanted before, but now those things were no longer a possibility for him. His dreams of an athletic scholarship were gone. Because he was unable to refocus and pivot, he held on to expectations that could no longer be obtained. He became discouraged and depressed.

Unfortunately, his story is a tragic one. He was unable to focus on anything other than what he lost. Thinking about the things he could no longer do became very painful. He started looking for distractions to take his mind off his unmet expectations. He found distractions in the form of alcohol and drugs. The substances would take his mind off the problems long enough to numb him. The unmet expectations were still there, and now he had addiction to deal with as well. He tried to get sober many times, but the reminder of his limitations hurt too much. As the drug and alcohol abuse continued the limitations became greater. And the vicious cycle continued.

We often begin to look for distractions because we are unsure of how to process our emotions.

There are thousands of stories just like this one. If only we could teach people to pivot, to let it go and move in a new direction. To stop saying why me? And start saying, what can I do with this? What a difference we can make in the world!

So how do you know if a distraction will work, or if you need to do the work to process your emotions? While there is no way to know for sure, I do my best to determine ahead of time if I think the feelings will persist. If you are wondering if it is time for a distraction, try asking yourself; how will I feel about this in an hour? In a day? In a week? In a year? The longer you think the emotions will be with you, the more strategic you will need to be in processing those emotions.

There are some things that we clearly have an emotional attachment to, and ignoring it will not make it go away. So, what do you do when the distraction is clearly not working?

If you find that your emotions are so strong that a distraction is not effective, there is only one other option and that is to do the work to process that emotion in a healthy way. That is what the 4 D strategies are designed to do. You will learn strategies to process your emotions. You will also learn strategies to manage the emotions that will never go away. Nothing will ever cause me to forget about Abby, but I have learned to carry those emotions in a healthy way.

Chapter 5

Oh, the Drama

Have you noticed that some people who are stuck tend to have a lot of drama in their life? Not you of course, but I'm sure you know people like this. They seem to feed on attention even if it is negative attention. Drama is defined as an exciting, emotional, or unexpected series of events or set of circumstances. When there is drama it means that everything surrounding your circumstance becomes a big deal.

We thrive on drama because of the emotional highs and lows. A change in your emotional state is a change in your physiological state. According to noted neurologist Antonio R. Damasio, (https://www.scientificamerican.com /article/feeling-our-emotions/) emotions are the body's reaction to stimuli. Sometimes it is an external stimuli and other times it is can be simulated in the brain by remembering an event or by showing sympathy for another's emotion. If we do not go through emotional and physiological changes, we start to feel bored or stagnant or emotionally numb. The change helps us feel alive.

We consider people to be dramatic when they frequently have an emotional crisis. This happens because they repeatedly allow themselves to get into the same circumstances that yield the same negative response. Or because they feed on the attention they get from a personal crisis. Quite often they are making their circumstances out to be a much bigger deal than they really are.

I was interested in learning more about this connection between emotions and drama, so I decided to go right to the source. My fellow unstuck speaker, Sheryl Green and I, had the privilege of spending a day with television and movie director Mark W. Travis and his partner Elsha. My expectation was that we would learn a few things about how important emotions are to the success of a movie. What we got was an experience. Mark and Elsha are amazing people with a very keen awareness of emotions and of self.

Elsha asked me if I knew where emotions came from? I admit that I was confused by her question at first. Then she walked me through an experience. Emotions are indeed a response to stimuli. As she talked to me I started to feel my body changing. She would ask me questions that seemed odd at first. She asked me how my spine felt about the work I was doing with Unstuck? I thought it was a silly question, then I felt myself start to sit up a little straighter. The feeling of pride came over me as I sat taller. This was cool, I could feel that emotions do come from the body, but I still wasn't sure what that had to do with drama.

When I told Mark about my 4D strategies to living unstuck he told me that what he does is the exact opposite of what I teach. It was fascinating to learn about his process. Mark has a program to teach other directors how to apply the Travis Technique. He told me that most directors will tell an actor that they need more of a particular emotion; more sadness, more anger, more rage. He said this usually causes the actor to do the same thing, just louder. Mark does a few things different. He talks to the character, not the actor. While I teach people to manage their expectations, Mark exaggerates them. The more grandiose the expectation the better. Once he gets the character to buy into that expectation then they replay the scene. He says that they end up with a raw, real emotion. Sometimes it is a different emotion then they had expected, but it ends up being a genuine response, making for a much better scene.

Think about yourself in the movie about your life. If you were to greatly exaggerate the expectations you have for yourself, and you got the same results you are living with now, how different would you feel? By exaggerating the importance and significance of an event or outcome you are increasing the drama. In other words, you are creating your own drama.

I have someone in my life that is very important to me. It is very hard to have a conversation with him. Everything in his life is extremely important. Because his expectations are exaggerated there seems to be a great deal of drama when things don't work according to his plan. The problems intensify because he thinks that everyone around him should care to the same degree that he cares. Because the people around him are not as disappointed as he is, he feels like they are somehow responsible for his pain. By exaggerating his expectation, he is creating drama in his life. Because the people around him are unable to meet his expectation they find themselves being drug into the drama as well.

This type of drama makes for an intense scene in Hollywood. Unfortunately, it also makes for intense scenes in our homes as well. We can tolerate drama in the movies because we know that at some point the character will find a greater purpose and will shift his focus from the problem to the quest. In the end they will emerge as the hero.

Mark led me through another exercise. He had me take on the character of a writer. The writer I was playing was a great writer and my partner. My character was named Mike. Mike talked about what he would have done better if he were writing this book. Mike would have done a few things differently. Mike would have written a better book. Then he involved Sheryl. Sheryl got to talk directly to the character, Mike. She helped me see how to bridge the gap between Mike and John. When I returned home I began rewriting this book. I was determined to write up to Mike's standards.

Mark and Elsha reminded me that there are different characters living inside of each of us. We get to tell our bodies which character will play which scene in our life story. I could play the role where I am a victim. I'm a lonely introverted kid. I have a car accident that leaves me unable to walk for a year and with permanent pain. I then lose my mother, my daughter and two more failed pregnancies in the same year. Then I end up divorced and alone. I have lived a very sad movie. Or I can play you the role where I do not let anything hold me back. I work hard in recovery to walk again after the doctors told me I would not. I lose my mother and daughter but then use that as inspiration to become a writer and start a business to help others learn to live unstuck lives. That shy introverted boy is on stage motivating hundreds of people. And I get married again and live happily ever after. There is a hero and a drama queen alive in all of us. They are fighting for prime real estate in your mind. The one that wins is the one you feed.

By learning to manage your expectations and applying some emotional intelligence you can do some editing to the movie of your life. You can be a drama queen, or you can be the hero of your life story. You can tell your body how to feel or you can allow your circumstances to tell your body how to feel.

Drama can definitely make your life more interesting. I do not believe that all drama is bad. Just be aware of when the drama is real and when you are creating drama through unrealistic and exaggerated expectations.

To be completely honest, my business is dependent upon drama. I host conferences for people who have had major trauma in their life, they share what has happened to them, and what they did to get themselves unstuck. I am responsible for selecting the speakers for each event. When I first started I just called some friends who had great stories. As the conferences became more popular, the demand to be on stage increased. I now must go through an extensive selection process to determine what the line-up of speakers will be for each conference.

I hate to tell people no. I believe that everyone should be able to share their story. But the reality is that we only have time for so many speeches, and it is up to me to maintain a certain standard. The standard, drama! I need people who have stories that will engage the audience and send them on an emotional journey. I have found that it is the emotional journey that leads to the break throughs. Remember that we get stuck because of emotional issues. I could stand on stage and give people solutions all day long, but unless I can get them to feel, the solutions are useless.

For us to have a great event, and bring about the change the audience desires, I need the audience to laugh a little, cry a little, laugh some more, and leave feeling inspired. That is the formula that I have found to have the greatest impact on people. Our aim is to help people move beyond their circumstances.

To put on a great event, I need to have the right mix of stories from the speakers. I never thought, in my lifetime, that I would ever have to say these words, but I did, "I'm sorry we cannot use you for this conference, we already have someone who lost limbs, but we will call you for the next one." Ouch, that was hard to say, but a great event requires the right mix of stories.

Just like the movies, I have control over where the drama will lead. I know that the people on stage are sharing emotional stories, but I also know that they are not stuck in those emotions, and I know that they will not leave the audience stuck either. When I see an audience start to cry I do not worry, because I know they will laugh again soon and they will leave feeling inspired.

While drama does make life more interesting, it is important to make sure that you maintain some control over how much you allow the drama to impact your life. Just like in the movies, be on the lookout for the turning point in your life story. Find your quest and start out on your hero's journey.

The rest of this book will give you strategies to help you process your emotions in a healthy way. There are a couple of things I can suggest now to help you avoid over exaggerating your expectations.

Take a minute and observe an object in the room you are in now. Notice how small the object is in comparison to the surrounding environment. I am looking at a water bottle across the room. As I look around the room the water bottle does not appear to take up much of the volume of the room. Now concentrate your focus just on the object and not on the environment. As I stare at the bottle it starts to appear bigger. Suddenly the bottle takes center stage and the room around it becomes blurred. The more you focus on something, the bigger it appears. In much the same way, when you focus on your problems, or what you do not have, it appears bigger than it really is. It is said that drama is making a mountain out of a mole hill.

When Mark turned me into Mike the writer instead of John. I realized that John had some insecurities that were holding him back. There are stories that I tell myself that makes me believe that I am not good enough. Remember that there are many characters living in each of us and the one that grows is the one you feed. Our insecurities stem from the messages that are replaying in our subconscious minds. Because we are not even aware that these messages are playing we allow them to continually loop in our minds and attack our conscious. To help you become more aware I have designed an exercise.

I refer to the messages that play in our minds as commercials. The commercials are always playing. In a moment I will have you close your eyes for one minute and think of nothing at all. But try to remember everything that comes to mind. After a minute you may open your eyes. Ready, go.

If you did this exercise successfully you should have seen many things. I saw at least 50 different images in my mind. Some good memories, some bad and some really random things. Try this a few separate times. Before each time try to call on one of the characters inside you. I thought about Mike the writer and the images that came to mind were stronger more powerful than previously. I thought about a time when I felt insecure. This time the commercials that played reinforced my feeling of inequity.

Think of your brain as a cable box. When you watch tv there are hundreds of channels sending signals to your tv, but the cable box helps block the other channels, so you can focus on one. Try to focus on the character you would like to play the hero of your story and block out the character that plays the drama queen.

Another fun fact that I learned about drama; ... The **term** "**drama**" comes from a Greek **word meaning** "action" (Classical Greek: δρᾶμα, **drama**), which is derived from "I do". If you ever wondered why we have drama in our marriages it is because we have requested it at the altar, when we said I do.

The next time you start to feel like you are taking on drama, remember this. The heroes in the movies go through some of the same processes that we go through. They have an unmet expectation that causes them to have an emotional response. They get stuck in their emotions. Then they apply the 4 D strategies we are about to uncover. Let's read on to see how you can be the hero of your story.

Chapter 6

Strategy #1

Deal with your unmet expectations.

Have you heard any of these before; "just deal with it", "get over it", "look on the bright side"? These are all statements that people make with the intent of being encouraging and supportive. The problem is that while we are in the midst of our circumstance we are not able to process this way. They are cognitive solutions to emotional problems.

When I was a kid my mom used to ask me a question, (I believe it came from an old poem, I have tried to source it but too many people have taken credit), she would ask me "where does the white go when the snow melts?" This is a fascinating question to a kid. Children live in a world of possibilities, yet at the same time they require an explanation for everything. From a logical perspective I knew that the snow is white and therefore, when it melts it should leave white residue behind? Okay I may not have said residue as a kid, but where did the white stuff go? I have since learned that the white we see is a reflection and when the crystals are no longer there, there is nothing to reflect. Okay, but where does the white go? Adults would attempt to explain the crystallization process and the reflection to me, but I had such an emotional attachment to the white snow that I could not grasp the cognitive explanation.

Deal with it, get over it, and look on the bright side are all things that I know I need to do in order to move on with my life and find happiness, but what do I do with the emotions that are attached to the circumstances? Do they just disappear? Or are they mere illusions like the white of the snow? If I get over it, where does the hurt go? In my case if I could just deal with it and get over it would I never hurt anymore over the loss of my mother and my daughter? Could I look on the bright side and forget that there ever was a dark side? It would be great if we could just flip a switch and turn our emotions on and off, but it does not work that way.

In my corporate speeches I often use cups to attempt to explain positive psychology, how it works and why it fails. Positive psychology teaches us to look on the bright side, just choose to be happy. It teaches things like the law of attraction and the secret. Positive psychology teaches us to do the things that are positive, in order to change our perspective. To demonstrate this, I have a cup that I refer to as my happy cup. (I use a clear mug.) Then I take a picture filled with colored liquid to show how I pour positivity into my happy cup. I could wake up in the morning and listen to uplifting music, read, pray, meditate, exercise, talk to a friend. There are lots of things I can do to fill my happy cup. If you make a conscious effort to pour positivity into your happy cup throughout the day it can alter your state of mind, making you happier.

These are all great things and I can see how positive psychology can be helpful. Why I believe it falls short is because there is another cup. This cup holds all our hurts, hang-ups, and heartbreaks. All of our unmet expectations go into this cup. I refer to this as our misery cup. We rarely pay any attention to this cup. We stuff it all down and pretend that it is not even there.

Throughout the day our souls thirst. We need to draw from our happy cup. We are constantly withdrawing and replenishing the contents of our happy cup. The levels in our happy cup are always changing.

The reason why positive psychology works is because what is in your happy cup hides what is in your misery cup. The problem is that if you never do anything to empty the contents of your misery cup you will eventually have to pour positivity into your happy cup all day long just to be able to get through the day.

I recommend that you continue to do all the things that positive psychology teaches you to do. I would also suggest that in order for those things to be effective, long term, you must do things to empty the contents of your misery cup. Strategy one, Deal with your unmet expectations, is all about emptying the contents of your misery cup.

I mentioned earlier that we get stuck because of the emotions we have attached to our expectations. I have identified four major emotions that are typically associated with the contents of our misery cup. What I mean is that our unmet expectations create one or more of these emotions. We hold on to these emotions as long as we allow them to sit in our misery cup. I realize that there are many emotions, but I have found these four to be most prominent. The four emotions are fear, frustration, anger and depression.

Fear – This occurs the moment that you realize the status quo is in jeopardy. Something is about to change, and that change could be painful. There are many circumstances that could illicit fear.

Frustration – We get frustrated when things are not going our way, especially after we have put forth effort and are not yielding the results we expect.

Anger – Anger is a strong feeling of rage. Typically associated with circumstances that are unfair or painful. Often accompanied with blame for a responsible party.

Depression – I love what the comedian Stephen Wright has to say about depression. He says that depression is just anger without enthusiasm. When we feel depressed we often want to be mad but we think, why bother nobody will care anyway. When someone feels depressed they often compensate by lowering the value they place on outcomes. They just stop caring or care much less than they once did. This is often a coping mechanism to lessen the effects of unmet expectations.

All of these emotions are normal natural emotions. It is okay to feel these emotions when faced with difficult circumstances. What is not okay is to sit in them for too long.

Before learning to apply the strategies in this book, I spent way too much time sitting in my own misery and not dealing with the contents in my misery cup. So much so that my misery cup was overflowing. I was doing all the things I was supposed to do. I went back to work. I was exercising. I was going to church. I was doing everything I thought I was right. I was filling my happy cup and I thought it was working. I didn't feel like there was anything wrong. I certainly did not feel depressed. Now I can see that I was suffering from what I now refer to as a functional depression. Just like a functioning alcoholic, I was able to perform my regular tasks without any difficulty. I thought I was doing fine but everyone around me could see differently. I was alienating the people around me. I had a short fuse, I became frustrated and angry easily. I took any constructive feedback as a personal attack. And even though I was eating the same way I always had, which was horrible but still the same, and was exercising every day I still gained 50 pounds. My body was trying to tell me that it was in an emotional overload.

It wasn't until I found myself divorced and sitting alone in my misery, having alienated everyone around me, that I decided I could not continue with life this way. Something had to change. That was when I started writing. Two weeks later I had my first book, "Finding Your Happiness".

My first book was the beginning of my journey. The start of my new life. I will spare you all of the details of my journey and skip ahead to the strategies that have helped me and countless others. When you master these concepts, I am certain you will be able to live like there is nothing holding you back.

I had mentioned that the unmet expectations in our misery cup have negative emotions attached to them. The process of understanding these emotions and which emotions we tend to emit, is the basis of emotional intelligence. In the beginning of this book we stated that we are all the sum of our 3 E's, education experience and emotional intelligence. You can improve your emotional intelligence by developing an awareness of self and of others.

If you were to evaluate each of the items in your misery cup, every unmet expectation that you have, and try to determine which emotions each one elicits, you will begin to see a pattern in how you process emotions. For example, when I did this exercise, and wrote out each unmet expectation, I learned that I was prone to become frustrated and sometimes angry. I rarely felt fear and never felt depression. The same exercise with my wife revealed her tendency to feel depressed when things do not work out. I discovered that most people have a go to emotion, an emotion that surfaces more often than others.

By understanding that I am prone to frustration and anger, it has allowed me to recognize the onset of those emotions and revaluate that expectation. It allows me to pivot and move in a new direction before becoming engulfed in the negative emotion. It also helps me to see how others process emotions. Now at the first signs of depression in my wife, usually unordinary silence and distancing, I'm able to redirect the conversation and hopefully prevent that depression from taking root. Part of dealing with an unmet expectation is knowing what that emotion is capable of doing to you. It is no different than going to a doctor for an antibiotic at the first signs of an infection. The doctor knows that if left untreated that infection could be deadly.

Now we understand these emotions and how they affect us, but we still have not actually done anything with those unmet expectations. Which means that we are still carrying the negative emotions around with us. We are going to look at 5 things that you can do with those items in your misery cup.

1. **Forgive others.** When you hold on to your hurts, hang-ups and heartaches you are agreeing to carry those negative emotions around with you. You tend to feel as though others should carry the burden for you because of the role they played in the outcome. The reality is that as long as you have unresolved issues with others, you are being weighed down by the emotions surrounding the circumstance. By forgiving others you are not admitting that you were wrong, or they were right. You are not even saying that you are okay with what happened, or that you are willing to mend the relationship. All you are agreeing to when you forgive others is to stop carrying around the weight of the emotions. You are dropping the issue, so you do not have to carry it anymore. The beauty of that is that they do not even need to be notified that you forgive them. Forgiveness is not about them it's about you.

The difficult thing about forgiving others is that it releases them of the responsibility for your negative emotions. It took me years, but I had to finally forgive everyone in my life that I thought was holding me back. They were no longer responsible for my feelings. Once I forgave them for holding me back, I quickly realized that they were not holding me back at all. What was holding me back was the fact that I had not dealt with my unmet expectation. By forgiving them, I back free to move. I was no longer being held back.

2. **Forgive yourself.** I often find it much easier to forgive others than to forgive myself. Many people carry around a great deal of guilt and shame. This is because you know that your actions in the past were not in line with your core values, often resulting in hurting others. I admit to holding on to guilt. There are some things that I have done in my past that have resulted in hurting people I cared about. Some of those hurts I am certain are still sitting in other people's misery cups. I have a hard time forgiving myself because I feel bad for causing emotional hurt. The truth is that there is no amount

of feeling bad that will make the situation right. Feeling bad has never changed the past. The only benefit to guilt is that it prevents you from making the same mistake again. Holding on to guilt can also prevent you from being the change you were meant to be. Guilt is what tells you that you are not good enough. That's somehow the world will not accept you because of something you have done in the past.

I believe in God and in spiritual warfare. I believe that there is an evil force that wants to prevent us from doing good in this world. I have no doubt that the greatest weapon that evil force has is guilt. If we only knew how many great men and women were on course to make a difference in the world only to be thwarted by self-doubt as the result of guilt and shame. I do not intend for this to be a religious book, but I have to say that God has forgiven you, what makes your judgement greater than His? Forgive yourself so that you can free yourself of the guilt and shame that gets you stuck.

I wish I could tell you that I have mastered the art of self-forgiveness. What has helped me in this area is to do much like the exercise Mark W. Travis did with me. I had to acknowledge that there are different versions of me. In order for me to be the best version of myself I need to forgive the version that committed the shortcoming. I still do this regularly. There are times when I feel sorry for myself for not reaching a certain level in my career or finances. It is in those moments that I have to call on the version of myself that has accomplished a lot in a short amount of time. The better version of me forgives the version of my that is not living up to my expectations. Then I let the better version take over for a while.

3. **Let it go.** No, I am not a fan of Frozen, but I think that girl is on to something. Sometimes we need to be willing to just let go of some of those expectations that are no longer capable of becoming a reality. I had to let go of the thought of ever playing competitive sports again. I also had to let go of my dreams of a modeling career. Just kidding. As circumstances change our expectations need to change with them. The funny thing about letting go of a dream, it frees up your hand to catch a new dream.

Here is a little secret about letting go of a dream. When you let go of a dream it leaves a void. That's why tragedies are so hard to get over. That void often hurts. I have seen too many people let go of a dream, only to keep looking down at it. They are like a little kid that dropped his ice cream cone. They just keep looking down. They are stuck. They key to letting go is that you must quickly pivot. You must turn and move in a new direction. Forget about that old dream and step forward in faith believing that things will work out. If you do this, I promise you it won't be long before you have a bigger and better dream.

4. **Use it for good.** This is when you are able to take something out of your misery cup and put it right into your happy cup. I think of my friend Dustin. He was in an accident that left in paralyzed. Dustin started a foundation to aid in the research of spinal cord injuries. He is using a tragedy in his life to positively impact others.

Most successful people will tell you that they are grateful for the trials and tribulations they have endured. It is those things that we think will ruin us that define us. When we are able to start asking, "what can I do with this? instead of asking "why me?", we will begin to see opportunities to turn our pain into positive.

The Bible promises us that God can work all things together for good. Not that all things are good. I believe that in every hurt, hang-up and heartache, there is a lesson to be learned. There is something that you can use to help yourself, or someone else later on.

5. **Not yet.** Let's face it we all have things that we are just not ready to deal with yet. There are things that will stay in your misery cup until you are ready to deal with them. And to be perfectly honest there are some things that I never want to get over. I don't want to get over my daughter. I want to remember her. I want to stay in touch with all the emotions I felt while she was here with us. I do not want to get over some of the things that have made me who I am today, as painful as they may be. In those cases, I agree to allow those items to remain in my misery cup. In order to allow this, I must

resolve to do the work on a regular basis to empty the remaining contents from my misery cup, making it possible for my happy cup to achieve its purpose. Not everything can be dealt with right away. If there are things that you are not ready to move out of your misery cup, that is okay. Just make sure that you acknowledge that it is still there. By acknowledging it is still there, it will help you to understand where your emotions are coming from and may help you to manage them better.

There is one more strategy for Dealing with your unmet expectations that I would like to recommend. This is specifically for those items you are not ready to deal with yet, or may never chose to deal with. It is an unusual concept that I created but it has done wonders for me. I call it **"scheduling my pain."** That's right I schedule pain.

Put it on your calendar to go feel bad. If you do this every occasionally, it gives you permission to feel. It is an opportunity to stay connected to the emotions that have defined you.

When I schedule my pain, it is a time for me to think about my daughter and my mother. I think about all the hurts, hang-ups and heartaches that I am still carrying around with me. I allow myself to feel all the emotions associated with these events. While it gives me permission to feel bad it also allows me an outlet. I recommend that you always do this in a park or someplace away from your home. I know that when I leave the park I can leave the emotions behind. I know I will be back there again someday. In the meantime, it allows me to take the positives I have learned from those experiences without being weighed down by the negative emotions. Essentially, I am paying respects to the painful things that have made me who I am today, without being stuck in them.

It is my sincere hope that you will take the time to deal with the contents of your misery cup. If you do the things I recommend in this chapter you will feel lighter and more free than ever before. This is the beginning of the transformation to living an unstuck life.

Chapter 7

Strategy #2

Define Your Ideals

We have heard for years how important it is to have written goals. It is also well documented that people with written goals tend to be more successful. I believe that it goes much deeper than just writing down some goals. I have found that successful people have a <u>crystal-clear</u> <u>vision</u> of what they <u>expect</u> out of <u>life</u>. There are some key words that I have underlined in this sentence.

There are four things about the sentence that go beyond just writing down some goals. It starts with getting crystal clear. Successful people know before they begin what the outcome will be because they have seen it in their minds eye a thousand times. It is not enough to say that you want more money, or you want to help people. Successful people can tell you how much money they intend to make and how many people they will help. They have a crystal-clear picture of who they serve and how. This is important because most people speak in very general terms. They know they are not happy with their current situation, but they are unable to identify what will satisfy them. The more crystal-clear you can get about your expectations, the more likely you are to achieve them.

I remember going with a friend as she began shopping for a new car. She would say that she was just looking to get ideas because she was not sure of what she wanted. She just knew she needed a new car. As we looked at cars I could see that she knew exactly what she wanted, she had just never taken the time to process it. We would look at a car and she said no, she wants an SUV. We would look at an SUV and she would say, it must have a third row of seats. We found one with a third row, but she insisted on cloth rather than leather seats. We found one that met that description, but it wasn't red. How much easier would it have been to walk onto the lot and say that we were looking for a red SUV with cloth interior and third row seating?

This is a very common scenario. We are unhappy with what we have but have not taken the time to identify what we do want. We eventually uncover what we want through a process of elimination. I believe that we know deep down at our core what will make us happy, but we are busy processing what we don't want which keeps us from seeing what we do want.

I spent much of my life saying that I want to be happy, having no idea what that meant. When I started using the Personal Happiness Graph, I was able to see exactly what was going to make me happy.

That leads us to the next underlined word, vision. There is a definite difference between a goal and a vision. Vision requires some creative thinking. As an athlete we set goals at the beginning of every season. That was nice, it gave us something to work towards. I highly recommend writing out your goals. What seemed to work even better for me were the visualization exercises I did before each game. I used to hang my game jersey above my bed and fall asleep dreaming about seeing that jersey flying around the football field making big plays. I would also arrive early on gameday, put my headphones on and hit the field. On the field I would line up and run through plays all by myself.

At least to everyone else I appeared to be by myself, in my mind there was a team across from me and a stadium packed with roaring fans. Before the opening kickoff I had played that entire game several times in my mind. I had already been in every difficult scenario and have succeeded. I felt extremely confident that I was prepared to handle anything I was faced with throughout the game.

It is very important to have a big picture vision to accompany your goals. Think about what you would like for yourself and spend time visualizing yourself already having what you want. I recently had the pleasure of meeting a young man named Harlem. Harlem was in an accident that caused him to lose his eyesight for 7 ½ months. Harlem said that he was able to stay positive because even though he could not see, he had not lost his vision. You need your eyes to process sight, you need imagination to process vision.

The third underlined word is expect. That expectation signifies a belief that you are going to accomplish what you have set out to accomplish. When you are able to walk in confidence, believing that things will work out, then opportunities seem to just fall into place. When you hope or wish for things to work out, there is an uphill battle to fight. It seems as though you invite resistance. When you expect things to work out there seems to be much less resistance. Not to get religious on you, but I believe in spiritual warfare and the number one way to prevent you from achieving is to plant a seed of doubt. The most successful people do not hope to win they expect to win.

The last underlined word was life. What good would it do to have a successful book launch and still live a miserable life? The key to a happy life is to apply what you know across each area of your life. We are all experts at something. I believe there is a hidden genius in all of us. In order to expose that genius we must take a whole life approach, and not just focus on one area. Make sure you are taking the time to identify what you want in all areas of life. I recommend using The Personal Happiness Graph to help direct you. It is important to identify what will make you happy in each area of life. Too often we work hard to get what we want in one area of our lives only to be left incomplete because other areas of our life are not being satisfied. Make sure you are focusing on what you want rather than what you don't want.

I was about 5 years old when I received my first cap gun set. It was the coolest thing out there. There was a toy gun that looked like a real gun. It was heavy and shiny just like the real thing. The kit came with a badge, a bandana and a plastic holster belt. It also came with rolls caps. The caps were a red sulfur paper. You would feed the paper through the gun and when you pull the trigger the hammer would strike the paper. This would create a small puff of smoke and would emit a sulfur smell. (Yes, I grew up in the 70's and 80's, and somehow, we survived.) It was like I had just fired a real gun in the wild west. I mean this thing was cool for a 5-year-old! I was so happy with my gun that a year later I got the newest version as another gift. Even at 6 it was pretty fun. After my third gun set I started to get a little bored. After all I was now seven or eight, it was time to put those childish ways behind me.

When I was eight my grandmother took me shopping with her. It was early November. She told me that I had a cousin about my age that had a birthday coming up. She asked me what a boy my age would want. At this point I was over the gun thing. I was even a little annoyed that I received the same gift three years in a row, from different sources of course. My first thought was not a pure one. I said to her "apparently boys like this gun set." I thought if I got stuck with the same gift three years in a row it is time for someone else to get one. Looking back, I should have realized that the boy cousin closest in age was only 3, and Christmas was a month away. I'm sure by now you figured it out, she was shopping for my Christmas gift. My smart mouthed response was to blame for my forth gun set. So, my question to you is, are you so focused on what you do not want that it prevents you from seeing what you do want?

How do you do this? How do you develop a crystal-clear vision of what you expect out of life? There is a process to help you. I created the Personal Happiness Graph for just this purpose. It gives you a tangible representation of how happy you are with your life at any given moment. It illustrates the difference between your ideal self and actual self in the five main areas that encompass all your expectations. The top line of the graph represents a perfectly happy you, or your ideal self. The bottom line represents you right now, or your actual self. I have been using the graph to help people find happiness for twenty-five years now. It works every time because it is based on the value that you give to each aspect of your life. The graph is explained in detail in my book "Finding Your Happiness".

After you have completed the graph and assigned a value to each category, the next step is to define your ideal. In other words, what would your life look like if you were perfectly happy in each area of your life? The graph focuses on five areas; people, responsibilities, activities, money and environment. Any expectation we have can fall into one of those five categories. After years of trying to find an acronym for the categories, I placed a dollar sign for money and had PRA$E. This is what I was missing, PRA$E. For all of my OCD friends, I realize that I just used a dollar sign for an S. I'm okay with that. I have also had people call me and tell me that I need to add another category because there is an "I" in praise. My response is, "If I don't need praise, PRA$E don't need I." Let's look at the five areas.

People. What would your life look like if you were completely satisfied with the relationships in your life? I am not just talking about romantic relationships. Take some time to consider all the relationships in your life. I have created some workshops that take people on a deep journey to identify people in every social setting and determine what it would take to be completely happy in every setting.

Take some time and deeply examine the relationships in your life. Being around the right people is a major driving force to happiness, as well as success in any endeavor. Jim Rohn said we become like the five people we hang around the most. Who are your five? More importantly, who do you need to move out of your top five? In my workshops we look at where you are positioned in each of your social settings. The truth be told, we have some people in our lives who hold us back from being the best versions of ourselves. You can learn how to keep loved ones in your life, without giving them a seat at your top five table.

Responsibilities. Responsibilities are very important and often not recognized. When I say responsibilities, I am referring to the things that define your sense of purpose. We all want to feel like what we do is important, either at work or personally. What are you doing to make a difference? What would you like to be doing to make a difference?

Many of the people I work with tell me that they feel stuck in their careers. They do not feel like they have an opportunity to grow or advance. They use words like dead end job, and unsatisfying career. It amazes me how many people do not feel like their work is important. I believe that every job is important. If someone is willing to pay you it is because there is a value associated with the work you are doing. The real issue arises when we do not feel like we are recognized for our contributions, or when we are not able to utilize our gifts and talents optimally.

The people I have worked with who were most satisfied in their careers, were people who were doing work that they were uniquely gifted to do, and they could see how their gifts were directly correlated to the success of the organization they worked for. This was an even greater indicator than the amount of money they received for their work. It is a great feeling to know that you are bringing value to your organization.

It is worth noting that I did not say what the value was that they were bringing to the organization. All that mattered was that the person felt like they had a special skill that contributed to the success. That special skill could be their ability to sell, or to produce great graphics. It could be a cashier with a warm smile. You do not have to be an expert technician to contribute to an organization. You just need to know that you are making a difference.

If you are unable to use your gifts and talents at your current job, I urge you to find an organization you can volunteer with to put those talents to use. You will feel much better knowing you are making a difference somewhere with your unique skill.

I am reminded of a job I had years ago. I was a manager. We had been outsourcing all our graphic design work. One day I was in the warehouse talking with some of the workers there, when a gentleman was telling me how much he enjoyed helping his daughter create this flyer for a school project. The next time we had a flyer to create I went to the warehouse worker and asked him if he could create a flyer for us instead of outsourcing. He did. After he created a flyer for us guess what happened next? No, we did not move him to a graphics department, we still outsourced that work. What did happen was, he became a much better warehouse worker. Suddenly he felt a greater sense of purpose. He felt like he made a difference and that completely changed his outlook on his daily work and the company.

Take some time to acknowledge what purpose you would like to serve. I would recommend creating a personal mission statement declaring what difference you would like to make in the world and for whom? Mark Twain once said, "The two most important days in your life are the day you are born and the day you find out why." One reason we get stuck is because we are constantly trying to fit a square peg in a round hole. We are trying to be what others expect us to be rather than what we are uniquely gifted to be. When you find what you excel at and you use it for good you will be living unstuck.

Activities. Have you taken the time to identify what you like to do for fun? Are you doing those things? We get stuck in a rut when we are going through the motions of life and not doing the things that make us feel alive.

In twenty-five years of doing the personal happiness graph, I have yet to find someone who values activities and is living an active lifestyle, who feels stuck. If you are truly living your bucketlist lifestyle it is impossible to feel stuck. There was no better example of this then my dear friend Dale Krause.

Shortly after writing "Finding Your Happiness", I began doing public speaking events based on the book. I attended a networking event for speakers where I met Dale. He had just decided to start speaking about living his bucketlist lifestyle, while battling stage 3 colon cancer. In a short period of time Dale fell victim to the market crash and lost his home, he lost his business and he went through a divorce. Amid dealing with all of that, Dale was diagnosed with stage 3 cancer. Dale made the decision to not let his circumstances control him. He created a bucketlist. Dale started dance lessons and chemotherapy on the same weekend. He was determined to laugh and dance his way to recovery.

Dale beat stage three cancer and began speaking to people about getting off the couch and living life. He emphasized not waiting for a terminal diagnosis to start living your life. I can honestly say that Dale scored the happiest of all the people I have ever graphed. The number one item on my bucketlist today is one that Dale and I crafted together. He spoke with me at the first two Unstuck Happiness Conferences. Together we set a goal to hold an Unstuck Happiness Conference in all 50 states.

Dale Krause passed away in September of 2016. I was blessed to be with him in his last days. He was a man that was not afraid to die, but desperately loved living. I did not know Dale prior to his cancer diagnosis, but I knew him well enough to know that it was that terminal diagnosis that got him living.

Dale did not get stuck. He never allowed his condition to stop him from living an active lifestyle. He crossed off over 26 items from his bucketlist in the time I knew him. He had several reasons to feel stuck, but he never did. Instead he focused on his activities. In doing so, he was able to meet great people. By helping others understand the bucketlist lifestyle he gained a sense of purpose. He didn't worry as much about money and he put himself in environments he never thought were possible before he got sick. By increasing his activities, he narrowed the gap in every other area of his life. Dale was the perfect example of living an unstuck life.

We do a tribute to Dale at each Unstuck Happiness Conference, and his journey is part of the Learning to Live Unstuck documentary film.

Be careful not to fall into the same trap that many high-powered people fall into. I have done many graphs with people who rate responsibilities and money as very important and rate activities low in importance. They suffer from delayed gratification. They say things like, when the kids are grown, when I get a promotion, or when I reach this milestone; then I will do the things I want to do. I urge you start enjoying life now before it is too late. When you do that other things will fall into place as they did for Dale.

Money. Do you feel stuck because of your financial situation? Take the time to identify how much money you need, to live a completely happy life, rather than focusing on how much you have, or don't have. You will probably find that you need less than you thought you needed. We all say that we want more money, think about exactly how much more you would need, and exactly how you would allocate that additional money if you had it. I highly recommend taking a course on financial education to help you with this process.

Money is one of the major reasons why people feel like they are stuck. Interestingly enough, of all of the people I have worked with who were once stuck and now claim to be unstuck, there is only one who can contribute his transformation to money. That is only because when he was stuck he was homeless and living on the streets. He did not have the money to meet his basic needs. When he finally found work, and saved enough to get off the streets, his life began to change. Even he does not attribute the change in his life to the money. It was his servitude that actually got him unstuck. As soon as he could he began giving back to those less fortunate.

I mention his story only to illustrate that if you do not have money to meet your basic needs for survival then money can make a difference. For the majority of us, money will not solve our problems, or get us unstuck. That is not to say that people who get themselves unstuck do not make money. Many of them are very well off financially. But they will never say that the money is what has made them feel free. Money is simply the by-product of the work they have done to live unstuck in other areas.

Environment. The last category is environment, or your personal space. Take the time to think about your ideal environments. What do you need in your ideal environments? I'm using the plural because I want you to think about your home, your place of work, and anyplace where you spend a significant amount of time.

I have found environment to be one of the most under-appreciated categories. There has been a great deal of research on the effect of our environments on our mental health. They have found that clutter can play a significant role in anxiety and procrastination. It is difficult to be successful and feel like you are making progress while surrounded by clutter.

There are a number of items related to your environment that contribute to your state of mind. Subtle changes to your environment can make the difference between being stuck and being inspired. Some of the items that have proven to make a difference are lighting, color schemes, clutter, cleanliness and scent, just to name a few.

Do the work to identify what your ideal environments look like. Then take small steps to create that environment for yourself.

When it comes to living an unstuck life, it is extremely important to identify your ideals. It is also important to revisit them frequently. I have found that I often have to re-define my ideals. Sometimes our priorities change as our circumstances change. And sometimes we are forced to change our ideals. There are some things that I wanted out of life that are no longer possible. If I continue to want things that I cannot have, I will continue to be miserable.

I learned this the hard way. I was so excited when I found out I was going to be a dad. For years after Abby passed I was still wanting her here with me. Don't get me wrong. I would trade anything in the world to hold my daughter again. But the reality is that I cannot have her, not here on Earth. I will not see her again until I join her in heaven.

Instead of feeling bad about not being able to hold her, I had to redefine her role in my life. I spend time with her regularly. She is my motivation for everything that I am doing in my business. I now say that every day is take your daughter to work day.

It was not easy to let go of the dream of raising her. It was not easy to accept the fact that I will never play competitive sports again after my accident. It may not be easy, but I have found it necessary. Instead of feeling bad about what I do not have I try to find out how those things can be used for good. I redefine my ideals when the need arises.

I have known many people who are stuck because they are still looking at their circumstances and wanting the same things they wanted before the circumstances changed. Life happens. The most successful people are the people who are able to recognize when things need to change, and they pivot accordingly. They pick themselves up out of the wreckage of their lives, turn and look in a new direction and move forward in faith believing that things can work out. Moving in a new direction means that they have redefined their ideals.

Chapter 8

Strategy #3

Develop Your Faith

The third strategy is to develop your faith, or the belief that things will be okay. Faith is a very interesting topic. The dictionary defines faith as a high degree of trust or confidence. We usually associate the word faith with a religious belief. Faith is said to be believing in something that you cannot see. When we are faced with difficult circumstances I believe that it is important to be able to pick yourself up, turn and move in a new direction, in faith, believing that things will work out. It is then that opportunities will present themselves to you, but they will never meet you in the middle of the wreckage. But what does the in faith part look like?

When you are sitting in the middle of the wreckage of your life, it is very difficult to see past the smoke of your immediate circumstances. You become so focused on the pain that it often feels like it will be permanent. When you are ready to pick yourself up and start moving again it will require faith. It requires faith because you usually have no idea how things will work out, you just need to believe that they will. The premise of this chapter is that faith can be developed. What do you do when you are not confident that everything will be fine? Can you improve your confidence level and self-esteem?

I used to believe that confidence had to be earned. The more success you had, the more reason you had to be confident. It used to puzzle me how some people could have such high self-esteem without achieving an equivalent level of success. It took years of research and life experience to uncover the secret to self-esteem. I don't mean to be one of those guys that claim to have discovered a cure all, but it must be a secret or why would there still be so many people suffering from low self-esteem?

What I have found to be the number one trait in people with higher self-esteem, is a developed faith. I am not necessarily talking about faith in God, though that certainly helps. I am referring to the faith in knowing that things are going to work out.

I have identified four keys to developing your faith so that you can start living an unstuck lifestyle and accomplish more.

The first step to making any change is to understand where you are currently. To help you determine where you are with your faith I would like to introduce you to three of my friends. I bring them along when I speak to organizations. I use balloons to represent people and their level of faith.

The first is a yellow balloon with a smiley face. The yellow balloon represents a person who is happy most the time. They believe in all things positive and they have complete confidence. This person is accustomed to things working out. They know that everything happens for a reason and that pain is temporary. They believe in positive psychology and it works for them. Positive psychology works because they are able to empty the contents of that misery cup we talked about earlier. It is much easier to forgive and let go when you know that everything will work together for good somehow. The yellow balloon has a highly developed faith.

The second is the blue balloon. This person believes in all things positive. That is to say, they believe it is possible because they see it work for other people. They believe in positive psychology. They believe it in their head, they just don't feel it in their heart yet. This person wants desperately to be positive, but they wonder "when is it going to be my turn?", or "when is it going to work for me?". This is a very dangerous place to be. This is where self-doubt creeps in. You start wondering if you are good enough. You may even wonder if God loves you. I know this feeling far too well. I have spent a lot of time being the blue balloon. It is hard to be completely confident when you are faced with one trial after another. You want to believe but it is so hard.

It was exhausting, living as the blue balloon. I used to say that I was the optimistic pessimist. Today sucks, but tomorrow is going to be great. I wanted desperately to believe in the positivity, but I had a hard time facing the fact that my life was not what I had expected it to be. Fortunately, I did not give up and I eventually learned the strategies I am sharing in this book. Just keep believing and apply what has helped me and I am sure you will start to live unstuck as well.

And then there is the angry faced red balloon. This is the person who has had about all they can handle. They are tired of hearing that everything that goes wrong in life is because they willed it to be so. Like somehow the company they have been employed at for twenty years went out of business, and they got laid off, because they didn't write enough positive post it notes. Or a family member is suffering from cancer because they did not have a positive attitude. This is the person who, about the same time I said happiness is a choice, wanted to punch me in the face. They do not want encouragement they want solutions. This person has very little faith that things will be okay.

Not having a high level of faith is not a character flaw. We have a tendency to think that everyone is like us. We fail to realize that people process things differently based on their current level of faith.

When we see someone struggling we often feel inclined to help. Unfortunately, that help is not always as helpful as we hoped. For example, telling someone to look on the bright side and reminding them that everything happens for a reason and it will all be okay, will often not be well received. For the yellow balloon type, this encouragement is often accepted and appreciated. They get it. The same advice has a different effect on the blue balloon person. They often process that encouragement as a character flaw on their part. If everything works for good, then there must be something wrong with me because I am not experiencing the good. The angry red ballooned person may get even more angry then they already are. They are not ready to hear the positive yet. They often view the encouragement as one more person rubbing it in to them. I know that we are all well intended and want to help, just do not be surprised if your help is not openly accepted, based on the current state of faith.

The difference between the three people is the level of faith they have, or the confidence that things will work out in the end. Which balloon do you associate with? Are you ready to let go of that balloon?

Your level of faith is the result of your education, experience and emotional intelligence.

As children, we are either taught that everything will be okay, or we are taught to be afraid. If you do not do the right thing you will suffer consequences. That is motivation by fear. Fear has a way of blocking self-esteem. The two do not coexist, at least not as they pertain to the same circumstance. One will always be more dominant. What you have been taught influences how you view your experiences. When you fear that things will not work out you tend to fixate on the problems. The longer you stare at the problem the bigger it gets. Conversely, when you approach a problem with the confidence that it will work out, the easier it is to adapt and start moving in a new direction, taking your eyes off the problem.

You learn to have faith based on what you were told and what you observed. Your parents either taught you to fear or to be confident that everything will be okay. They also demonstrated for you. As the old saying goes, "more is caught than taught". Take some time to think about your parents or guardians. How did they handle adversity? Did they demonstrate fear? Or did they show you what it looks like to walk in confidence? Where did they learn it? Do you know how your grandparents handled adversity? You may have a long lineage of unlearning to do, but it is possible.

The second key to developing your faith is to surround yourself with people who have a highly developed faith. I recommend finding people who have been able to overcome difficult circumstances, especially if the circumstances are similar to your own. We mentioned earlier that Jim Rohn said that we become like the five people we hang around the most. Find people that you can relate to and can have a positive impact on your well-being.

You can often borrow the experiences of others to help you develop your faith. By listening to, or reading about people who have overcome great obstacles you can begin to see that things can work for good. That is why we all love movies, we like the heroes journey. The hero gets stuck, they show us their struggle to get unstuck. There is a turning point and the hero emerges victorious. When you spend time immersed in a world of positive outcomes you begin to believe that it is possible for you too. If you don't believe me I dare you to watch a Rocky movie and not shadow box for a week. I don't think it can be done. You will begin to see yourself in the shoes of the hero.

I developed the Unstuck Happiness Conferences because I have been blessed to know some amazing people who have overcome tremendous circumstances. I wanted to provide an opportunity for them to share their stories and strategies with others. Through sharing stories, the speakers are reliving their success and the audience gets to add the experience of being an eye witness to that success. Every success story we share helps to increase the faith of the people we share that experience with. By developing faith, we are positively affecting self-esteem.

If you are surrounded by negative people, or people who live in fear, it will be impossible for you to gain a heightened sense of faith. If you are not sure how to find positive people just start asking. You can do a google search for inspiration. I have found it helpful to join groups such as toastmasters, or community organizations of like-minded people. You can search meetup groups or community calendars for groups in your area.

Another way to surround yourself with positivity is to embrace positive psychology. While I do believe that you must work to empty your misery cup, it is equally important to fill your happy cup. Take some time to do the things that will add to your happy cup. Do things like listening to positive uplifting music, talk to encouraging friends, read, pray, meditate and exercise. By partaking in these activities, you will find yourself surrounded by other positive minded people. In return you will see your confidence level adjusting accordingly.

I can honestly say that the reason I can hold my head high today is because of the inspirational people I am surrounded by on a regular basis. As a football coach we used to tell the kids that attitudes are contagious. Ironically, in that world I was not surrounded by the attitudes I wanted to catch. It was by entering the world of public speaking, and finding a church community, that I was exposed to attitudes that were worth catching. If it were not for the people I met in those arenas I would still be alone in my misery.

It is also important to note that your family and friends may not always be your best source of inspiration. Often the people that have cared about you your whole life, want to protect you. That does not mean that they understand you, or what you are trying to make out of your life. I am not suggesting you cut them off, maybe just be careful of how much of your dream you share.

I am a believer in recover groups and therapy, but I do believe that they are only a piece of the puzzle. Self-reflection is great, but it often keeps the focus on the problems. I believe in picking your head up and focusing on creating a new future for yourself. There are millions of resources available to help you on your journey. But I am sure I am preaching to the choir as you are already reading this and taking action.

When done correctly self-reflection and therapy lend themselves to the third key of developing faith and that is your personal history of success.

One of my favorite movies is a Disney movie, The Kid, with Bruce Willis. In this movie Bruce Willis's character is about to turn forty when he meets a boy that turns out to be himself at the age of eight. At one point the eight-year-old turns to the forty-year-old and asks, "what happens next, between being me and becoming you?". The forty-year-old version goes on to tell the eight-year-old about a series of events that led him to his current life. While watching the movie it occurred to me that we all have stories. We have all had moments where we felt stuck, and it seemed as though things would never get better.

The third key is something that I have based on a workshop exercise that I created. It requires taking an inventory of past events. Unlike other programs, I will not have you focus on what happened and what you did to get over it. All I want you to do is acknowledge the struggles you have had. I usually have you complete a timeline. We go back in time and uncover what your biggest struggles were and what emotions were attached to them. We go back to a point in time and have you discuss what you were dealing with at that point in your life. We do this for several different periods in your life.

I do not have you dig up the past to examine it. I simply use it to prove a point. Most, if not all, of the things you were once worried about are no longer worries for you, at least not to the same extent. The things that you once thought would last forever have become distant memories.

Then I have you take the time to write a personal letter to yourself as a child. In this letter you will talk about all the things that you have dealt with in your adult life. Notice that I said things you have dealt with. What happens during this exercise is, you begin to see that you have made it through some difficult times in your life. The fact that you have survived some of those circumstances is proof enough that you can survive whatever circumstances you are facing today. By writing to yourself as a kid, you find yourself assuring the kid in you that things will get better.

We are rarely dealing with the same problems we had five years ago. That means that five years from now we will have a new set of problems. That may not sound comforting but just knowing that the things we feel consume us today will not even be issues in the future, makes it easier to process them now, and lessens the impact on our emotional well-being.

The eight year old version of me would have never guessed this life was possible. If I knew then that I would have the life I have now, I would have had a lot less to worry about.

This leads me into the forth key to developing faith and that is understanding emotional intelligence. When we talked about dealing with unmet expectations we talked about processing four emotions; fear frustration, anger and depression. If you recall, we talked about taking all our unmet expectations and creating piles based on the emotion each circumstance evoked. We have found that we have a tendency to elicit some emotions more than others. Each of us process our emotions in a different way. One person is more likely to get angry, while another experiences fear. Emotional intelligence is the ability to recognize your emotions and the cause thereof, and an ability to recognize emotions of others.

Understanding emotional intelligence is critical to developing your faith. It is impossible to walk in confidence when you are overwhelmed with feelings of fear, frustration, anger or depression. Don't get me wrong, we all experience these emotions that is just a normal part of life. The problem is that we cannot be truly confident while we are immersed in the emotion. That is why there is no such thing as a person who is completely confident all the time. We all find ourselves dealing with emotions. An understanding of how you process your emotions can help you get those emotions under control so that you are able to walk in confidence.

Let me give you an example of how I had to develop my faith recently. I have spent much of my time as the blue balloon. I was very optimistic about my future success, I just had no idea how I would achieve success, or when. I am also prone to feel frustration as my main emotion. Knowing this about myself, I set out to host an event much larger than any undertaking I had previously taken on. I knew deep down that this event had the potential to be awesome, but I was not completely confident that it would turn out that way.

I knew what had to be done, in order to pull off a great event, but I was not sure if I had what it takes to make it happen. I was experiencing both fear and frustration. I knew that fear was not one of my normal emotions, but this undertaking was much greater than anything I had done before. Therefore, I had fear that I would not succeed. That fear was rooted in potential financial failure as well as possible public embarrassment. I knew where the fear was coming from so I dealt with it as good as can be expected. It was my frustration that kept rearing its evil head. Several times throughout the planning process I ran into issues or unmet expectations. I was expecting things to just fall into place and when they didn't frustration showed up. One of my biggest frustrations was knowing that other people did not seem to care as much as I did. I wanted everyone to be excited about the event. I expected everyone to be promoting the event and selling tickets.

It became obvious that I was getting stuck in my frustration pattern. Ironically it was in the process of planning an Unstuck conference. I took a very deliberate approach to developing my faith while preparing for the conference, once I realized I was getting stuck.

The first thing I did was realize my pattern of being the blue balloon. I was hopeful that this would be an awesome event, but did I really believe it deep down at my core? The answer was yes. I did believe this would be an awesome event and once I said that out loud I was able to shift my perspective. When that self-doubt began to creep in I reminded myself that this event was bigger than me. I acknowledged that my doubt was not strong enough to stop this from being great.

Next, I surrounded myself with people who could encourage me, people who had done what I am doing. I have a couple of friends who have done events in the past and they were instrumental in my process of developing faith. They shared with me some of their struggles and successes. I was able to see that I was on the right track, I just needed to keep doing what I was doing. It helped me to know that they faced adversity along the way, but they were able to succeed. I cannot express enough how grateful I am to have found people that can relate and can pour into me in this way. I became an eye witness to their experience which helped me realize that it is possible.

The third key was to take an inventory of my past. Although I was not where I had hoped to be in my career, a quick inventory of what I had accomplished in a very short time proved valuable. In just a two-year period I had written two books, hosted a radio and television show. I had done numerous appearances on television and radio. I had performed keynote speeches for various groups and I had begun the process of filming the Learning to Live

Unstuck documentary movie. This may seem like I am bragging about my accomplishments. The truth is I was using those accomplishments to try to prove to myself that I was capable. I had done things that many people could not or would not do. Now I do not think that I am any better than the next person, I am just determined. It is important to note that I did not go around telling people about all these accomplishments, at least not until just now. These were words of affirmation I used in private to negate any negative self-talk I had been experiencing. And yes, I was experiencing plenty. I needed to convince myself that I was worthy.

And finally, the forth key, I had to put my emotions in check. I knew where the fear was coming from and I knew that the frustration was created in my own mind because that was how I was used to processing. I was able to evaluate those emotions and see them for what they really were, unmet expectations. When I began to feel the emotion coming on I asked myself, what expectation do I have that is not being met?

When you have an unmet expectation, there are two things you can do. You can do something different to get what you want, or you can change what you want. When I felt that emotion coming on, I would assess whether or not that expectation was worth holding on to or just let go. If it was worth holding on to I would figure out what I had to do differently. There were some expectations I had to just let go of, like the expectation that everyone would work as hard as I was working.

As I adjusted my expectations things changed. While the event was not as financially successful as I had originally hoped, I can honestly say it was one of the most amazing events I have ever attended. My faith was tested along the way. Lucky for me I was aware of what I needed to do to develop that faith.

It is my hope that you can take my experience and use what I have learned to help you. You are now an eyewitness to my success and I hope that you can pull on my experience to develop your faith. There is nothing special about me or my ability. I have just put myself in the position to learn from some incredible people. By following these four keys you can expect to gain a greater confidence too.

Chapter 9

Strategy #4

Drive-On

"To continue in a course of action even in the face of difficulty or with little or no prospect of success", this is the Oxford Dictionary's definition of the word, persevere. This also defines everyone who is living an unstuck life. There is an enormous sense of gratification in knowing that you have faced adversity and you did not give up.

Driving on is easy to do when you have momentum. It is when that momentum stops that we get stuck. When things get difficult we begin to look for an easy way out. We settle for the path of least resistance, even if that path takes us further from our dreams. It is easy for us to say it wasn't meant to be, or my priorities have changed. This world is full of incredible people and great ideas. It is my belief that the real tragedies of life are not the things that get us stuck, but the very fact that we allow ourselves to stay stuck, preventing us from reaching our full potential.

I recently boarded a flight and sat next to a gentleman around my age. I was flying home after a week on the road speaking in some very rural parts of the country. The man turned and asked me, "is this your first flight?". I was taken back by his question. What on earth would make him think this was my first flight. Then it occurred to me, maybe it is his first flight and he was looking for a way to connect. So, I asked him if he flies often, he said "some... this is my second or third time on a plane". I was actually flying to my third city that week. At that moment I felt an overwhelming gratitude to be in the position I am in. It is a privilege to be able to travel the country speaking to groups of people. I get paid to travel and talk, that's cool. But it is very easy to lose sight of how cool it is. I find myself getting wrapped up in the details. I focus on the unmet expectations rather than the great opportunity.

On the same plane I heard another man tell someone that he was looking forward to seeing an ocean for the first time. I understand that we all have different dreams and different priorities in life. And I certainly do not feel like I am better than anyone else because of what I do. But I admit to pondering what greatness lies repressed in each man and woman who have forgone their dream for the grind of day to day life. I do not condemn being responsible. Taking care of your responsibilities is a must. But I also believe that we are responsible for our dreams as well.

Not all dreams are of selfish ambition. I believe that God puts desires on our heart. It may be to test our will, or because it is part of His divine purpose. When you are moving in the right direction He will affirm you. Too often we confuse affirmation with ease. We think that if God is in it things will come easy. Quite the opposite. When God is in it the enemy is out to destroy it. I do believe in spiritual warfare. A pastor friend of mine used to say, "if Satan can't make us evil, he will make us busy". He will make sure that you become too preoccupied with day to day life to be able of focus on the mission that God has put on your heart.

Do you remember the song, Life is a Highway, written by Tom Cochrane in 1991? You may remember the Cars version or more recently Rascal Flatts. Life is a highway and I wanna ride it all night long. What a great metaphor for life. We all find ourselves on this highway with grand destinations in mind. The highway represents an express route to your dreams. A life filled with happiness awaits you at the other end of the highway. The thought of being on that highway and going full speed ahead is a wonderful image.

Have you been on a highway recently? There is a lot of traffic. It seems that on the way to our dream we must contend with others and their dreams. We may have different dreams, but we find ourselves competing for the same resources. Someone is in our lane and it is slowing us down.

As you travel along life's highway you will notice that there are many distractions. The side of the road is cluttered with signs. These signs are there to get your attention. They remind you to refuel, to rest and to replenish. These are all necessary endeavors. In and of themselves they are no danger to you, they are actually helpful. The danger comes when you take the exit ramp towards the places these signs are pointing towards. When you exit the highway, you see all sorts of interesting sights. It seems the enemy does his best work when you are tired, hungry, and running on empty. It is here that you will find the distractions that will make you too busy to continue down life's highway.

These distractions usually take the form of something good, at least at first. It might be a nice new shiny car, or that beautiful woman that catches your eye. I understand that part of the journey is enjoying what life has to offer. There is nothing wrong with stopping to enjoy life. I think if we were to be honest we all intended to stop and enjoy life for a moment and then get right back on that highway. Then the busyness sets in. You need to pay for that shiny new car. You do not want to leave the beautiful woman. You start families and you settle into life. It all seems good at first, but you get stuck in obligations. After a while the thought of getting back on the highway starts to fade and you begin living a life of quiet desperation.

The good thing is that not everyone who exits the highway gets stuck. In my travels I have noticed that wherever there is an exit ramp, there is an on ramp close by. It is never too late to get back on the highway and pursue your dreams. Your dreams may change, as a result of your time at that exit, but you can get back on the highway and pursue your new dream. That shiny new car and a partner to share life with are often wonderful and can make the journey much more fulfilling. They can point you towards new destinations, never before considered. It is when you want to go left, and your partner or some obligation, is forcing you to go right, that you start to feel stuck.

I am not against stopping to enjoy what life has to offer. The key is to experience the things that will enhance your life. I say all the time that we are the result of the 3E's; education, experience and emotional intelligence. It is when we take those exits that we grow and develop the 3E's. Cherish those experiences and grow from them. Take them with you if you can as you continue down life's highway. My caution to you is to not get so wrapped up in the experiences of the now, that you lose sight of the future. I have seen far too many people live lives full of regret, due to moments in time when they lost sight of their dreams in favor of something that felt good for a moment.

Life happens and priorities do change. It is in moments like these that you must apply the 4 D strategies. If your priorities have changed then you must redefine your ideals. You should do the work to deal with the expectation you had to let go of in order to pursue the new goal. And you should consider how you will develop the faith that you need to make the necessary changes.

It goes without saying that the further you travel the more you will see. As you drive-on on life's highway you will pass many exits and see many opportunities. It is a well-known fact that people with a college education earn more than people without. What I find interesting is the number of people I know who have a college education and are working in fields completely unrelated to their degree. While the education is helpful, the greater benefit was that they stayed on the road. They were driving on towards their dream. As you travel towards your destination the road will often split towards new destinations. I believe that these college grads were successful because they were on the highway when they saw a sign for a new opportunity, so they simply changed lanes. The further you travel the more opportunities you will have to change lanes. Just think about how many more opportunities you will see if you drive to mile marker 200 as opposed to exiting the highway at mile marker 2.

The successful people I know are very well traveled. They have changed lanes several times. They have taken many off ramps but have always found their way back onto the highway. They have found success, but few have found success in the same destination they had originally sought. It is safe to say that the number one distinction between the stuck and the unstuck is the willingness to drive-on regardless of the obstacles they faced.

Make no mistake about it, the drive is not an easy one. The road is long and filled with obstacles. There will be times when life at the exit will seem much more appealing than the highway. I can promise you that the further down the road you get the easier the drive. You will become an expert at navigating. You will recognize when it is time to get off the highway and when to get back on. You will have plenty of opportunities to change lanes. And you will see some pretty cool things along the way.

Although you will become more skilled at navigating life's highways you will never be immune to its hazards. On your journey you will face roadblocks, detours and collisions. Learning to distinguish them and how to navigate them will make all the difference.

I have had to face many roadblocks in my life. A roadblock is when you are unable to travel any further. The road ahead of you ends abruptly. It is no longer possible to reach your destination, at least not for you. You may be able to see your destination. You might see other people who were able to get there, but that destination is no longer a possibility for you.

It bothers me to hear people say, "you can be anything you want to be if you just put your mind to it and work hard". That is simply not true. We are all uniquely gifted and talented, but we are not all created equal. There are some dreams that we are just not created for. Can you remember a time when you realized that your life-long dream would never come true?

When I was a kid I dreamt of being a professional football player. To be honest it was not so much a dream as it was an expectation. I just always assumed that I was going to play in the league. My reality was a little skewed. I was so certain that someday I would play college football and then in the NFL, that as a kid I did not like to wear clothing with a team logo on it because I was afraid I would end up playing on a different team, as if somehow, I was being disloyal to my future employer.

During my senior year of high school, the letters came pouring in from colleges across the country, but the scholarship offers did not. The message was clear. I was a good football player, but I lacked the size and speed I would need to be taken seriously by division one schools.

Many asked me to walk on, but none took the chance to offer a scholarship. I went on to play division III ball, and I was pretty good, but I had to let go of any thoughts of playing in the NFL. My journey to the NFL hit a roadblock. It was no longer an option for me. Not making it to the NFL may have been the end of that road, but it certainly did not have to be the end for me. I simply pivoted and began moving in a new direction.

Someone recently asked me what my biggest regret was? I had to think long and hard. There are many things that I had wish I had done differently, but I can clearly see how all the roads I have traveled have led me to this place in my life where I am today. I am in a good place in my life now and I am using all my experiences for good. I have faced many road blocks and had several doors close on me, some by my doing, others by chance. But I am thankful for those experiences because they have made me who I am today. The only real regrets I have are for those times when my actions have harmed others. And there are a few. If you learn to pivot and move in a new direction you will find yourself exactly where you were meant to be. There will be no need to regret turns you have made because every turn has led you to the place you are right now.

You will face many roadblocks throughout your journey. Will you pivot quickly, or will you sit and stare at the roadblock wondering what went wrong? Admittingly I have done both. Remember, a roadblock is a barrier that prevents you from reaching the outcome you were expecting.

I can recall a time when I faced one of those minor roadblocks. It was dinner time and I decided to stop at Arby's for a roast beef sandwich. After all Arby's is famous for their roast beef. I remember it vividly. I was in Arizona. I approached the counter and placed my order. "I'll have a beef n cheddar" I said to the teenager behind the counter. He stared back at me as if he knew he was about to crush my dreams. Empathetically he said, "I'm sorry sir we just ran out of roast beef". What! Out of roast beef! This is Arby's, right? America's Roast Beef Yes Sir. How can it be that Arby's is out of roast beef? This was a road block because no matter how hard I wished for roast beef there was none to be had in that restaurant at the time. So, I got chicken instead! Interestingly enough, as I waited on my chicken sandwich I was comforted by a table tent. I was in Arby's in Arizona when I first learned that the very first Arby's ever, was actually in my hometown of Youngstown, Ohio. Had I not pivoted and changed my order I may never have known that fact. That was a minor road block. It was an unmet expectation but not one that I had placed a high value on. In this situation it was easy to pivot. It required very little thought. It is when we place a high value on the outcome that we often struggle to pick ourselves up, pivot and move forward again.

It is when you refuse to pivot, you sit staring at the roadblock, still wanting what you cannot have, that you find yourself stuck. Such was the case when my daughter passed away. I wanted a baby so badly. When we lost Abby, I was devastated. I tried to forge my way past the barricade. We even got pregnant two more times in that next year, each ending in an ectopic surgery. God had closed that door, but I continued to try to pry it open. I found myself asking, why me? I sat in my emotions for way too long and did not deal with them. I just pretended they were not there.

I thought that I would find happiness through being Abby's dad. When she passed away I thought I would never be happy again. The dream I had of raising her and watching her grow up had been taken from me. If you want something bad enough and you work hard for it you can have it right? Wrong. There was nothing I could do, no amount of hoping or praying that could bring my girl back to me.

Eventually I realized that I had to pivot. I could not go on wanting something I could not have any longer. It was time for me to change what I wanted and pivot. That may sound insensitive or cruel. Trust me it is not, it is simply a reality of life. I did not stop loving or missing my daughter. I just made a decision not to sit in my misery any longer. It was time to turn in a new direction. In doing so, I redefined Abby's role in my life. I made her my why for my business. I think of her every day, but I no longer ask why me? Instead I take the lessons I have learned and apply them to helping others.

Sometimes what looks like a roadblock is nothing more than a detour. In the case of a detour the destination is still available to you, but it is going to take you longer than expected and you are going to have to go through some things first. Life may take you down some back roads, possibly to teach you a thing or two before you arrive at your destination.

Many of us come to an end in the road and we assume it is a roadblock when it is actually a detour. You walk away feeling defeated. You give up on our dreams too soon. It could be that you did not recognize the detour as an option. It could be that you lost faith that things could work out because they did not go as easily as you had hoped. It could be that life got in the way and you turned to the safe route to meet your obligations and ultimately give up on the dream.

My journey with Unstuck has been a very interesting one. It is amazing how often during the process of planning an Unstuck Happiness Conference, I have found myself stuck. I have faced several obstacles along the way. I started Unstuck because I saw a need and I believed I had a model that could serve that need. My why was so strong that I was determined to find a way to move forward even when it seemed impossible. I am not a gambler, but I do love college football. I placed a college football bet and won. I knew that I needed to find a way to launch this business, so I took my winnings and rented a hotel conference room. I had a great conference but no profit. It was obvious that there was a demand for another conference, but there were no funds available to make it happen. I had hit a roadblock. I could see that I had to let go of my dream of continuing to hold Unstuck Happiness Conferences.

I found myself staring at the roadblock trying to determine

which direction to turn. I thought my goal was no longer an option but was not sure what to do next. So I did nothing. Fortunately, I was traveling the highway towards becoming a full time professional speaker. It was on that road that I met some amazing people who had been on the same road longer than myself. It was my good friend Darren LaCroix who helped me see that the obstacle in front of me was not a roadblock, it was a detour. I could still put on a great conference, I just needed to find a new creative way to fund the event.

I have learned not to accept a roadblock until I have thoroughly examined the situation and am certain that it is not a detour. In other words, I am sure that I have exhausted all my options and there is no other way for me to achieve my goal.

Even in the case of a detour you will still need to pick yourself up and move in a new direction. This time the direction change is necessary to get you back on track.

Although I would like things to happen smoothly and easily, I can honestly say that I am so thankful for the detours I have had to travel in my life. I have a greater sense of pride and accomplishment when I reach my destination after being detoured. The struggle and lessons learned on that dirt road have enhanced my experience. I also feel a greater sense of accomplishment because I know that many people would have quit when they saw that the road ended. Few people will find the detour and continue to drive-on.

As I mentioned, I do believe in God. I believe that there is a higher power. I also believe that there are times when that higher power will do something to get your attention and drag you to your knees. These are the collisions I spoke of. These collisions happen when you least expect it. It may happen in order to prevent you from continuing down the road you are on, so you can avoid destruction later on. It could be to get you to realize that there is an even greater opportunity if you are willing to look in a new direction. The thing about collisions, they are usually painful and life changing.

My car accident and the loss of my mother and daughter were collisions. They were painful events that have forever changed the course of my life. Those experiences hurt. In the midst of those trials, I felt all the negative emotions we discussed earlier. I would not wish for anyone to have to experience those emotions. However, years removed from the collisions, I am extremely grateful for the trials I have faced, and the emotions that have made me who I am today. I can now see how these collisions have forced me to move in a new direction. I was reluctant to move at first. When you find yourself forced to move in a new direction, embrace it. Years later I am living a life I never dreamt possible. I am helping people and it feels great. This life would never have been imaginable had it not been for the collisions in my life, and a willingness to keep driving on.

John Polish

Chapter 10

Unstuck, now what?

There is a difference between living unstuck and living a happy joy filled life. Nobody says that they want to live unstuck, we say that we want to be happy. When I began writing and speaking it was based on my book, "Finding Your Happiness". To me it made sense to talk about happiness. I had been unhappy for most of my life, then I experienced the loss of a child which took me from discontent to functional depression. The fact that I was able to pick myself up and find happiness again was something worth writing about and speaking about. Happiness is such a hot topic because we all want more of it.

My book and my speeches were very well received. However, I uncovered two facts that caused me to shift my focus from happiness to living an unstuck life.

The first thing I noticed was that some people who are unhappy with their own lives have a false sense of what happiness looks like. I encountered far too many people who were walking around with huge smiles on their face and extreme suffering on the inside. I did not want to be one of those guys that sells happiness. To me it is more important to help people actually find it.

Society has an expectation of what happiness looks like and it is completely inaccurate. The tragic suicide of comedian Robin Williams has opened our eyes to this reality. Few people could have suspected that someone whose life was laughter and smiles could be suffering from a mental illness. On the flip side, I had people question why I was not walking around smiling and cheerful all the time, since I wrote the book on happiness? Is it possible that someone could have a stern look and still be content with their life?

Our society has become desensitized. We have more ways to connect with people than ever before, and yet we are the most disconnected we have ever been. While technology has contributed to many great advancements in our society, it has also succeeded at isolating us more than ever before. This isolation has made it difficult to stay in touch with our own emotions, let alone be able to read the emotions of those around us. No surprise, just look at social media. Some are spending a great deal of energy trying to get others to see how wonderful their life is. While others are airing their dirty laundry hoping for online sympathy. I love what Les Brown had to say about sympathy seekers; "80% of people don't care and 20% are glad it's you." When you establish a higher understanding of your emotional intelligence you will experience less of a desire for external validation.

I am a living example, If I were able to take you back in time, about six years ago, before I began looking at emotional intelligence, you would see a very different person. Back then I was extremely moody and impatient. What I have learned is that my mood was often dependent on the immediate feedback of those around me. My circumstances dictated my happiness. If I received recognition for my work, I was motivated to do even better. If I received negative feedback at work, I would become disgruntled and discouraged. The same was true in my personal life. My mood would change several times a day. I was on an emotional rollercoaster.

I am not a doctor, but I am now married to one. I can tell you that constant changes to your emotional state are not healthy for your system. I experienced rapid weight gain as well as chemical and hormonal issues, as a result of the stress put on my body from the constant change of emotion.

Now that I have a much greater understanding of emotional intelligence, I'm able to recognize when my emotional state is changing. I'm able to process those emotions much quicker. Now that I know that the emotion is a result of an unmet expectation, I can apply the 4D strategies in this book to manage my expectations. As a result, I have become more self-assured. Because I have more confidence in my ability to manage my emotions I am less dependent on others to validate me.

I can promise you that emotional intelligence does not happen organically. It will take a concentrated effort to learn and experience how to process your emotions. I recommend attending some workshops designed to help you process your emotions. At Unstuck we host regular workshops to help you learn to live Unstuck. Emotional intelligence is a large part of that process.

The second, and most important reason for the shift from talking about finding your happiness, to learning to live unstuck, is because I found that it to be impossible to find happiness while you are stuck, and most people who were searching for happiness were indeed stuck.

I was hosting workshops on Finding Your Happiness. The workshops were well attended, and people were talking about how great they were. Attendees seemed to genuinely enjoy the content and left feeling inspired. I felt great knowing that I was able to impact people's lives. After a while I began to run into past attendees and I noticed that there were only a few who had truly experienced life change. The others experienced a temporary shift but did not result in any lasting change. Bothered by the outcome I began studying what was actually holding people back. I found that people were not able to let go of the emotions that resulted from past unmet expectations, which prevented them from moving forward. They were still stuck.

What I learned was that I had audiences filled with blue balloons. Remember the blue balloon represented the people who believed in their head, but were unable to feel it in their heart yet. These were the people that wanted badly to believe that my message would have a lasting impact on their lives. They were doing the things they were supposed to do to fill their happy cups, and it would work for a short time. Then day to day life sets in, and the issues and emotions are still sitting in that misery cup.

Those negative emotions; fear, frustration, anger and depression, can be repressed. They are very susceptible to distractions. You may have a fear that you are not going to have the money to pay rent. This fear is very real and very serious. You can sit with a friend and watch a funny movie. I may walk in and see you laughing and enjoying yourself while watching the movie. It may appear as though you are not living in fear over not having rent money. That fear is still there and is very real, but it is repressed for a while as you are distracted by the funny movie. I could have delivered the most motivational speech of all times and it would have had no results if the audience was still anchored by fear, frustration, anger or depression.

The positive emotions that distract us will quickly fade when faced with another unmet expectation. I have seen people sit through a moving and inspirational church service and then moments later experience rage over poor service at lunch. If you have not learned how to process your emotions, then the negative emotions will resurface each time you experience an unmet expectation, regardless of how happy you think you were just prior.

A few years ago, I had the honor of attending a lantern festival. This was an amazing and emotional experience. Ten thousand people gathered in the middle of the desert with lanterns. We would write our hopes and dreams, prayers and praises on the lantern and then light the lantern and watch as all ten thousand lanterns would ascend towards the heavens in a beautiful display. If you have seen the movie Tangled, then you know the type of lantern festival I speak of. It was one of the most remarkable sights I have ever seen. It was an evening filled with love, hope and positive vibes. Until...

They did not allow cars in the desert, so to get all ten thousand people there they offered shuttles out to the site. The shuttle ran all day, taking people out to the location. It was a good plan for getting people there, not such a good plan for getting people back to their cars. The event ended suddenly, and all ten thousand people descended upon the buses at the same time. The love, joy and hope were quickly exchanged for those negative emotions. The same people that were sending positive thoughts skyward were now kicking in the mirrors of the buses as they passed.

This is why positive psychology alone is not enough. We must master our emotional intelligence before we can move on and find happiness.

I knew that the only way I would be able to help people find happiness would be to teach them how to live an unstuck life first. Living unstuck is all about processing emotions. Successful people are able to walk in confidence. Confidence cannot coexist with the negative emotions, at least not while the negative emotion is prominent. It is impossible to be anchored in fear and confident at the same time. You cannot be depressed and still be certain that things will work out just fine. The only way to experience real happiness is to learn how to process your emotions first. Once you have dealt with your unmet expectations, defined what it is you really want, developed the faith that it will all work out, and committed to driving-on no matter what obstacles you face, then you can start to think about finding happiness.

The good news is that much of the work you have done to live unstuck can serve as the ground work for finding your happiness. Once you feel the freedom of living unstuck you will find it much easier to develop a plan for happiness. I would suggest that once you get unstuck, it is a good idea to redefine your ideals. The things you thought were important to you often change when you are not being held back by your negative emotions.

Emotional intelligence is not a tool to help you become successful and wealthy. It is a way to stay in touch with the truest version of yourself. In doing so you can stay in touch with the emotions that define you, without carrying them around with you. It will help you to experience the good things of this world while keeping all emotions in their proper perspective. The Bible says, "what good is it for you to gain the whole world but lose your soul". (Matthew 16:26) Many people have become successful because they learned to turn their emotions off. This may help them become successful, but they will never feel the joy that accompanies success.

Remember the children we spoke of in the very beginning of this book? They have it figured out. Children are happier because they live in the moment. They are not burdened by all the expectations. They still believe they can fly. Have you seen a child cry? Yell? Laugh? Of course, you have. Children are very emotionally expressive. They deal their emotions as they feel them. We can learn so much from children. Children utilize the 4

D strategies without ever thinking about it. They deal with unmet expectations, as they are quick to forgive and forget. The redefine their ideals. If they do not get what they want they may cry, but only until they find something new to want. They have a developed faith, mostly because they have parents and guardians that protect them. And they drive-on. Children are very persistent when they find something they want. Maybe it's time to bring out the inner child in all of us.

It is my hope for you to gain the desires of your heart. I want you to be able to walk in confidence. I hope that you maintain an emotional intelligence that will allow you to experience life to the fullest. And I pray you will have the wisdom to recognize the emotional needs of others, and the compassion to help satisfy those needs.

May you learn to live unstuck and find your happiness!

And remember;

> As long as you are willing to work the gas pedal,
> God can work the steering wheel,
> But He doesn't move parked cars!

Ways to work together!

- Contact John Polish if you would like him to come speak to your organization.

- Hire John to teach a Living Unstuck course, or Finding Your Happiness course to your group.

- Take advantage of online courses and training programs.

- Look for an Unstuck Happiness Conference coming to a city near you.

- Help us organize an Unstuck Happiness Conference in a city near you.

- Attend one of our annual Living Unstuck Summit weekends, which are topic specific.

- Support the documentary film Learning to Live Unstuck.

- Become a sponsor and partner with us to help others Learn to Live Unstuck

www.JohnPolish.com

www.UnstuckConferences.com

Unstuck
Happiness Conferences

AT Unstuck Happiness Conferences our mission is to inspire you to move beyond your circumstances and live like there is nothing holding you back.

We bring together people who have faced adversity and have emerged as leaders. The Unstuck Happiness Conference is a full day seminar open to the public, where experts share their struggles, strategies and successes.

You will laugh, you will cry, and you will leave inspired!

Our bucket list goal is to host an Unstuck Happiness Conference in all 50 states. We want to help people across the country learn to live Unstuck.

We are always looking for people with great stories to share. You can contact us to nominate someone with a great story.

We are also looking for cities to host an Unstuck Happiness Conference. If you would like to see an Unstuck Happiness Conference near you, let us know!

Find us on social media or at

www.UnstuckConferences.com

About the Author

John Polish suffered from what he now refers to as a functional depression. He has experienced a great deal of tragedy in his life: a car accident which left him unable to walk for a year, the loss of his mother to a sudden heart attack, the loss of his only child "Abigail" to a genetic disorder, two more failed pregnancies and a divorce, in a very short time. All while working in an unsatisfying career.

John is now an expert at turning pain into positive. He inspires people through his books and speeches. John is the founder of the Unstuck Happiness Conferences. His conferences bring together people who have faced great adversity and have emerged as leaders. They share their stories in a public seminar to teach people that they do not need to stay stuck in their circumstances. John and the Unstuck Happiness Conferences are the feature of the documentary film, "Learning to Live Unstuck".

John was born and raised in Youngstown Ohio. He holds a B.S. in Business Administration from Youngstown State University. He moved to Las Vegas, NV in 1997, where he earned his Masters' degree in education from the University of Nevada Las Vegas. John spent 17 years as a teacher and a football coach before becoming a full time professional speaker.

Already an internationally recognized author, he has written: *Finding Your Happiness* and *A Healthier Happier Business*. He also hosts Unstuck-TV.

John serves on the board of directors and hold the positions of academy dean and vice president for the National Speakers Association, Las Vegas Chapter.

John also founded the Unstuck Foundation, which is a non-profit organization to help people overcome tragedies and to teach people how to start sharing their stories to help others.